t'ree tins of **TURPENTINE**

t'ree tins of
TURPENTINE

*Dirt poor and Irish in Sixties Leicester –
one family's true story*

By
Tim O'Sullivan

Copyright © 2022 by Tim O'Sullivan

All rights reserved. No part of this book may be reproduced or used in any manner without written permission of the copyright owner except for the use of quotations in a book review.

Colour Hardback Edition 2023:
ISBN: 978-1-7395848-3-2

ISBNs
978-1-7395848-0-1: paperback
978-1-7395848-1-8: hardback
978-1-7395848-2-5: eBook

About the Author

Tim O'Sullivan is a former refrigeration engineer, who went on to build a successful refrigeration and air-conditioning business, a property company and is now owner of The Addies Pub in Leicester.

Tim was forced to grow up at 16 when he became a teenage father. His part in a failed armed robbery landed him his first of two prison sentences. On his release,  he discovered the mother of his child had moved on, and his son had a new makeshift father.

Tim went on to have two more children, Ryan, and Kelly, with his devoted wife, Pam. He reconciled with his oldest son, Lee, and turned his life around for the sake of his family. Tim landed a job in refrigeration and worked his way up, acquiring the knowledge and business acumen to grow and sell his business before developing a property portfolio and buying his local pub.

Tim picked up a dictaphone and recorded his memories for over a decade. He was encouraged to turn the recordings into this book to be enjoyed for generations. His memoir encourages us all to think about the stories we pass on to our own families that shape who we are today.

Mary, Mam, Tim, and John

This book is a collection of stories from my childhood and growing up around Leicester.

In 2008, I started using a dictaphone to record my memories, hoping to turn it into a book for my family and future generations of the O'Sullivans to enjoy.

It would not have been possible without the support and patience of Kate Myers. Thank you for helping me to make this happen.

I hope you enjoy reading T'ree Tins of Turpentine as much as I enjoyed writing about the highs and lows of life in Leicester as a dirt poor Irish boy who came good in the end.

Contents

PART ONE

Tim Joseph Patrick O'Sullivan 1
Nora McCarthy 5
Ireland and John 9
St Patrick's Church, School, and Our Street 15
Our House and Life in General 21
Black Sheep, Blind Dogs, and Christmas 27
Communion 33
Summer 39
St Pat's School 43
The Den 51
The Pub and Lewis's 55
Holidays 61
Home and Mablethorpe 67
John's Leaving 73
Back to School 77
English Martyrs 81
Getting On 87

PART TWO

Getting Ahead of Myself 93
My Skinhead Days 97
Margate 103
Further Education 107
Spring 1970 113
Wormwood Scrubs 117
Borstal 123

PART THREE

Getting Sorted 137
The Long Stop 147
The Visitor 157
Settling Down 173
Roots and Farewells 183
Fresh Arrivals, Sad Departures 195
New Horizons 205
The Next Generation 215
Homeland 225
He Wasn't Heavy, He Was My Brother 235
Fresh Beginnings 247
Our History, Our Inheritance 251
Tim's Family Album 255

PART ONE

Chapter One

Tim Joseph Patrick O'Sullivan

My father was a giant of a man with hands big enough to dig the earth itself. For the first seventeen years of my life, though, I didn't know him. My mother was born Kathleen O'Callaghan on 24 September 1928 at Skibbereen on the south-west coast of Ireland. Kathleen had thick auburn hair, which sported a natural curl. She had a strong constitution packed into a compact five-foot-two frame. Kathleen eventually found herself far from the shores of her home in the middle of Leicester.

The story goes that my father waltzed into the Black Lion one day looking like John Wayne, Kathleen's heart-throb, and that's what caught her eye. She poured him a pint and there it all started.

They got a bit carried away some time in November of 1952 and five months later they got married in St Joseph's church, on Friday 13 March 1953. My father got drunk. He could drink alright – he once drank twenty-five pints. The twenty-sixth was poured over his head by my mother. He spent his wedding night in Charles Street police station.

'Lock me up. I committed the worst crime,' he said to the desk sergeant.

'Why? What have you done?'

'I've just got married.'

That was the start of my mother and father's married life. What with Friday the thirteenth and the police, it was not the best of starts.

In the summer of 1957 I was three years old and was running about with next to nothing on in the front garden of our new house at Birstow Crescent, Mowmacre Hill. My pants full, I tried knocking on the front door. No answer. Mammy must have been out the back, gossiping with Marie or Mrs Hedley, our next-door neighbours. So I took my pants off and pushed them through the letter box. My good deed done – Mammy wanted my pants when they got like that – I ran back to play. Stark naked.

Mammy was happy. We'd just got our brand-new three-bedroomed council house with an inside toilet and a bath. We'd come from a one-up, one-down, six in a block, with one tap and one toilet for the whole block. That was 1 Knight's Yard, Leaden Hall Street, Belgrave. I don't remember it, but she talked about it plenty.

'Jesus, Timmy, ye dirty thing,' she said, swinging open the front door and scooping me off my feet. She took me inside, sat me down on the draining board, cleaned me up, dressed me and put something on my back to keep the sun off. I heard a baby crying and looked over; it was Mary Bridget, my eighteen-month-old sister, in her pram.

'You go off and play and don't get into any mischief. I've got to feed yer sister,' Mammy said as she placed me back on my feet.

This was the first event that etched itself on my memory, and there it stayed. So there we were in this big house on Birstow Crescent, Mowmacre Hill – me, Mammy and Mary.

As the months rolled on, winter came. It was a different house in winter. It was a big house for a little fella like me. I remember climbing the stairs, eventually getting to the top, the toilet facing me. I thought I'd climbed Mount Everest. The house was freezing, semi-detached, up at the top looking down the rest of the street. Wind came from all angles. If I was crying in bed at night, Mammy would come up and say, 'What's the matter, Timmy? You cold?' She would throw another coat over me by the light from the landing. It felt like I was nailed down in a lead coffin.

Sunday was always a big day, oh yes. We were up early on Sundays. Wash. Best clothes. Walk down to Abbey Park. Off to Mass and then off to Nora and Mack's.

My Aunty Nora. If Aunty Nora was mentioned, we immediately thought of food. Good food. She used to cook for a duke in London. When we got to Nora's there'd be a big welcome. She was a small, stocky woman with a broad Cork accent. Mack was a quiet man. We'd go in and Mack would make a fuss over us and sit us down.

I can't stress it enough: the great thing about Nora's was the food. She knew how to cook. She'd spend hours cooking the Sunday dinner, which was beautiful. And apple pie after. We would eat and eat. If you couldn't manage your vegetables, you wouldn't get any pudding. We'd sit down and sleep in the afternoon. Mack would go down the pub, then come back and we'd listen to the radio. Then we'd head home. We'd get the bus home; it was too far for us to walk – about four miles to Mowmacre Hill from Nora's house on St George's Street. The bus dropped us off at the terminus and we'd soon fall into the house, exhausted.

Tim's mother's family prior to the orphanage, in good times when his grandfather was a sergeant in the Garda. The Callaghan family: Mam, Grandad, Grandmother, Billy, and Bridget.

Chapter Two

Nora McCarthy

May O'Callaghan (my mother's mother, my grandmother), met William O'Callaghan some time in the 1920s, probably as the Civil War went from raging to simmering. William O'Callaghan had been a police sergeant in the newly formed Gardai in the fledgling Republic of Ireland. He was born in Cavan, May was born in Skibbereen, so how they came to meet can only be surmised. William had made his way to England to work and perhaps it was there that they met, married, and in a few short years had three small children. William died in the 1930s in Burton-on-Trent, exactly how is not known, but he would have been only a young man.

May made her way back to her hometown of Skibbereen and spent the next few years there, where she met another man. He wanted to take her to London, but he didn't want to take the children. A short while later she delivered her children in the middle of a rain-drenched night to the nuns.

It was a dark night when May O'Callaghan arrived at the orphanage with her three young children, Kathleen, Bridget and Billy. The rain smacked down as they approached the grand doors.

The children were just five, four, and three years old. They had taken the bus from Skibbereen and arrived late at night. Whether the children were crying, too scared to speak, or unaware of what was to happen, was buried in the past. The nun opened the creaking door and ushered them inside.

'I can't cope,' May said to the nuns. Three children, the rain still dripping off them, were taken from her and that was the last my mother ever saw of her own mother. That was 1934, and an Irish orphanage was not a good place to be in 1934.

Ten years later, enter Nora, Nora McCarthy. This is how the story goes: apparently Nora and Mack were on holiday back in Ireland on their annual return trip, visiting their usual haunts of Clonakilty and Skibbereen where Nora was from. For some reason, Nora found herself in the hospital, which stood high up on the hill in Clonakilty. Nora thought she recognised the young girl cleaning the ward.

'What's yer name?' she said.

'Bridget,' the slight young girl replied.

'Is it Bridget O'Callaghan? You haven't got a sister by the name of Kathleen, have ye?'

'Yes,' she said.

Amazingly Nora had known the girls' mother when she was living in Skibbereen years earlier and she knew that the young girls had been put into an orphanage. With thanks to God, for some reason Nora took charge and managed to arrange for Bridget and Kathleen to return to London with her and Mack, it is not clear what happened to their brother Billy but he didn't go with them. Bridget was sixteen and Kathleen, my mother, would have been seventeen. Nora herself was twenty-nine and was living in London with her husband Mack, like so many other Irish people pushed out of Ireland by lack of work. It would have been a monumental act to take on two young, traumatised girls and try to set their lives straight. Nora was no saint, and had no great fortune to share, but she knew a bit about suffering. She'd had seven pregnancies over the early years of their marriage, and had delivered seven lifeless blue babies. When any hope of having a family had seemed impossible, a ready-made one found its way to her.

My Mother Kathleen would tell stories of that orphanage and its strictness. They had to bathe with their clothes on, so they couldn't look at their own bodies. At Christmas they'd get one small present, an apple, an orange, or a doll if they were lucky – all things that had been donated.

One time she had been cleaning a room for one of the nuns. The table was laid with cakes and all sorts of treats for guests that they were expecting. Always hungry, Kathleen took one slice of cake. The nun found out. 'You'll pay for this dearly,' she told her. When Christmas came, the meagre presents were handed out. There was nothing at all for Kathleen.

Nora brought the two girls to Kilburn with her and Mack, then helped to get them jobs. The orphanage had taken its toll on poor Bridget. She couldn't hold down a job. Her experience of first losing her mother and then being placed under that strict regime had institutionalised her so that she couldn't cope with normal life. Mack found her a place in a convent in Brentford, London, where they catered for people like Bridget. There were a lot of girls in there with mental-health issues.

The convent was called Saint Raphael's; it was a great big Victorian building with high ceilings and cold, bare walls. It was run by nuns, who were very strict, and this suited Bridget down to the ground. She took up where she had left off in Clonakilty.

She was diagnosed with epilepsy, which wasn't properly understood in those days. It was eventually recognised as a neurological disease that causes physical and mental-health problems. Nora, Mack and Kathleen went to visit her often when they lived in London, and then every year when they moved up to Leicester years later. We carried on the tradition until she died, aged sixty-three, from untreated burns. Bridget idolised me and she wanted me to be a priest. Poor Bridget. So that was how Nora became such a big part of our lives – by chance.

Mack was born in 1893 in the old Cork debtor's prison. I took a tourist trip round it after it was turned into a museum. It was pretty grim, with a men's wing and a smaller women's wing. Women had to give birth in their cell, which was narrow and bleak. He was named Florence McCarthy (Florry). They must have run out of names, I guess. It would have been fairly memorable, and recorded, but a lot of records were destroyed in Dublin during the Easter Rising. Anyway, that was why we called him Mack.

Chapter Three

Ireland and John

I remember Mammy sitting me down one day. 'Now listen to me. I've got to go to Ireland to pick up your brother, yer older brother.'

I thought, *What do you mean, my older brother?*

'His name's John. He's been raised by yer grandparents, your dad's mam and dad.' I thought, *Dad? What's a dad?*

Tim O' Sullivan, my father, had left the farm where he grew up at the age of sixteen and headed for London, where he found work labouring in the building industry. One night, in Tottenham, he was attacked by six men, who gave him the beating of his life. He moved to Leicester and got a job as a miner. He worked round the pits in Desford, Nuneaton, and Coalville along with his mate, John O'Brien, who remained a long-standing friend. When the men came to enter the pit, the foreman used to do a breath test. If he smelled of drink, the foreman wouldn't let him in, and he'd be sacked on the spot. This happened to Tim around 1956. The marriage to Kathleen was stormy and often ended up with her grabbing us kids and dragging us all down to Mick and Helen O'Grady's on Kensington Street in town, long before we moved to Mowmacre Hill. Kathleen accused him of drinking too much. As a result of the arguments at home and after losing his job, Tim left town.

Kathleen had written to Tim's parents back in Gortahig, the farm in West Cork where my father was born and where all his brothers and sisters were born. Two of them died in infancy. Allihies was the closest village to the farm, which was in a wild, remote spot looking out towards Kerry, just twelve miles away over the water at the mouth of the Kenmare River.

I came across an O'Sullivan family history a few years ago and the genealogical research suggests that this branch of the family moved to Gortahig at the end of the Famine. My great-grandfather was Mike O'Sullivan, and he married Mary Harrington. They had fifteen children between 1883 and 1902. My grandfather, John, was the eldest son. Of the fifteen, nine chose to emigrate to the States. Most of them settled in Butte, Montana, because there were already cousins out there. Only one, Peter, chose to go to England. Grandfather John inherited the farm and married Mary Casey.

John and Mary had seven children who survived into adulthood. They were not as adventurous as their aunts and uncles. Six of the seven decided that England was a safer bet than the US. The four eldest, John, Mary Brigid, Margaret, and Kathleen, went to London. Tim, my father, followed, but had to be different; he ended up finding work in Leicester. His younger sister, Teresa, later joined her siblings in London. The youngest, Anthony, settled at home, married Eileen Lehane, and had two children, Mary and John.

With my father's older brother and four sisters married and settled in London, one wonders why my mother did not seek help from them first. Perhaps she had no way of contacting them, or knew they were not in a position to offer any help, just scraping by themselves and working all the hours God sent. With nowhere else to turn, my mother was determined that none of her children would feel abandoned and put into care as she had been.

In no uncertain terms, Kathleen let her in-laws know she couldn't cope with three babies on her own without their good-for-nothing son around. Out of guilt, perhaps, they agreed to take John until she got herself sorted out. That had to be better than leaving him with the nuns, and there'd be no fear about not being allowed to take him back. John stayed with them for four years and they grew attached – four years is a long time in a small child's life. He had learned to speak Irish, like them, and they began to think of leaving the farm to him.

My mother said she'd be in Ireland for two weeks and I was to stay with Aunty Nora and Mack. I thought, *What's Ireland?*

'I'll ring you every night.' She handed me a plastic toy phone and said I could talk to her on that. She kissed me and left. She must have taken Mary with her; I don't remember.

It was fun being at Nora and Mack's. They'd clear their throats and spit into the fire. If it was a nice day, there'd be no fire. There would be a newspaper at the side of the settee and they'd spit on that instead. They'd read and listen to the wireless.

Then, 'Yer mammy's coming home.' I'm not sure how Nora knew; she might have rung the local pub and got a message to Mack. Then we got ready for the arrival.

I was playing in the front garden; there were no fences – it was all open plan. Nora had taken me back to Mowmacre Hill. I saw Mam coming up the street with this lad, with John. I thought, *Jesus, look at the sight of that!*

He was ten months older than me. Mam had told me that at the old house in Leaden Hall Street, he'd slept in the top drawer, and

I'd slept in the bottom drawer. I thought, *How'd you get that lump into a top drawer?*

Anyway, he walked down the path. I was playing with a World War II ambulance pedal car.

'This is yer brother Tim, yer sister Mary, and Aunty Nora,' Mam said by way of introduction.

'Jesus, that looks like a grand car. Can I have a go at it?'

That was the first thing he ever said to me, then he wrenched me out of it by my arm and got in himself. After that scuffle, we went in. Nora made some tea and got some pie for John. Then she went off down the street to get back on the bus and go home. We waved her off. So there we were – me, Mammy, Mary and John.

Soon it was time for bed. He had to share with me, but John didn't like the dark.

John had a West Cork accent, like Mammy and Aunty Nora. He had spent his life back in Ireland on the farm with Grandad, fishing, and with thousands of sheep. And Grandmother idolised him. After breakfast she'd send him off, up into the mountains with just the sheep for company. He'd sleep with a candle in the room with Grandma.

When Mam went to the old farm to fetch him, John was riding bareback on a bull. And he didn't want to know. To him, Grandma was his mother. They reckoned there were terrible screams when the day came to leave. Mam had stopped there a week to try to get to know him again. I suppose, after three or four years, it had been too long. Grandma and Grandad were desperate by all accounts and pleaded with her.

'Please, please, please let him stay with us! You'll rue this one day.'

When it came time to go, he pulled away, throwing stones at her, and ran up the mountain. They waited until he came back. Bet he was hungry.

John was heading for England. He cried and cried, even when they got to the boat. It must have been a terrible journey. They had to travel from the further reaches of the area they call Beara of West Cork to the peninsula of Kerry, then Dublin to Liverpool. It would have taken twenty-four hours in a car; without one, it would have taken a couple of days. And there was John, screaming and yelling for his life all the way.

My, how my life changed after the arrival of John. That first night he cried and cried his eyes out. He had to sleep with the light on. It was a terrible shock for him – he'd never seen electric light. Never seen running water. That night was horrendous – he howled like a banshee for our grandmother. He would not go to sleep and Mam was in and out. I was trying my best to get to sleep with the light on. Mam was starting to lose her patience with him. Eventually he slept; he must have cried himself to sleep, I'd say.

In the morning we got up. Mam told me to wash my face and get ready for breakfast. John had never even seen a toilet. It was quite funny – he wouldn't go on it. In Ireland John's idea of a toilet was that you'd go out in the field. Dock leaf. Wee anywhere you wanted. So the laughter began.

John hadn't seen a flannel either. His idea of a wash was down in the river. Mam had to wash him all over with him screaming like a banshee all over again.

Toast was the order of the day. Every day it was toast. There was no stale bread in our house. The birds used to sit on the windowsill thinking, *You miserable tight bastards! Where's the crumbs? You're not even throwing out the stale bits!* If the bread went stale, you toasted it. John wasn't happy. That wasn't enough to feed him. He had three or four rounds of toast.

After breakfast, Mam pushed us out the door into the garden. That was our world. It must have seemed very small to John. He'd walked up mountains. He'd had thousands of acres. He'd had his own favourite places. And here he was stuck in this garden. He just couldn't cope.

They were building the shops. At that time there were temporary wooden huts that potential shopkeepers used about thirty feet from our front door. We weren't allowed out of the gate. Watching people wander by, John soon became very bored. And hungry. He was forever hungry.

Two or three weeks down the road, things hadn't improved at all. Mam was still holding him on the toilet when he was going for a bob. He'd be screaming his head off, saying the toilet was actually hurting him. Me and Mary, we'd be giggling at the bottom of the stairs. Every night we still had the light on. He still screamed for his grandma. And that was how things progressed for a few more months. Eventually, he did start calming down. Mam would wait for him to go to sleep and sneak in and turn off the light.

Chapter Four

St Patrick's Church, School, and Our Street

There was great news. Saint Patrick's was opening on Stocking Farm. The Murphy family had built it and paid for it themselves. The old one in town, next to St Pat's Club, was on its last legs. There was to be a brand-new big church dominating Beaumont Leys Lane.

Opening day was a big day, when the first Mass was to be said, so we were washed and dressed for it. There were hundreds and hundreds of people there. Mam was chatting to people with mainly Irish accents. St Patrick's church meant no more catching the bus or walking for an hour to get to Mass. This was our parish, and it played a major part in our lives. That was when Sundays changed, and sleepy afternoons at Nora and Mack's drifted into the past.

Mary was coming into her own then, talking. Our garden had been transformed. Mam had planted potatoes, cabbages, and peas along the side. The front section was long and open. Next door lived Marie and Jeff – we went to their wedding. We kids had never seen so much food in our lives. Custard. We got stuck into that. Marie had three daughters – Julie, then Elaine, then there was a big gap. Julie was my age; Elaine was Mary's age. A big gap, then Susan.

The wire fence at the back of the house was trodden down flat after years of going next door. They had a beautiful garden with roses and a lawn. She thought she was royalty. She worked in the day and part-time as a barmaid by night. She and Mam would gossip, gossip, gossip. Whispering, always in and out. Marie spent most of her time around our house.

On the other side of our house was Mrs Hedley, Miriam, a war widow. Her husband had been killed in the war. She had a daughter, Pauline, a lot older than us – a big lump of a thing she was. Mrs Hedley was only little, dainty, but both of them were nice women.

About halfway down the street were the Cannons. He was from Liverpool. They had three sons, older than us, two of them in and out of prison for burglary. Our front door was on the side of the house, facing in their direction. On that side we'd acquired another large patch of land, which Mam filled with potatoes, rhubarb and all manner of things. She made it beautiful. To the left of our door was a gap where the temporary shops were built, those wooden sheds.

Bill and Kathleen Murphy and their daughters Eileen, Kathleen and Maureen, and a little lad called Bill who was John's age, lived just over the road on Birstow Crescent.

That was our street.

John turned five in 1958, so that made me four, and Mary three. He had to start school. There was no sense taking him three and a half miles to St Pat's, so Mam sent him to the local school, four or five hundred yards away. Mary and I were still at home. We'd take him to school in the morning, all four of us. Drop him off, pick him up. I don't know how he got on there; I don't remember much really.

Then came the day when it was my turn to go to school. We went to Social Services, who gave us some coupons, and then we went to John Cheatle's in the high street and got a brand-new St Patrick's uniform for each of us. John was pretty tall now, a good foot above me, tall for his age. He was dreading it.

The O'Connors moved into the street; Mam knew them from the old days. They'd lived above a dry cleaner's in town until they got a house on Mowmacre Hill like us. They had a child every year. Sheila was the mother, a very religious woman, and one of Mam's best friends, and Billy was the father. Marion was my age; Bridget was John's. They just went down and down in age. She eventually had twelve children, but two died.

We'd go to their house, wait for them, then walk down the hill to the school bus stop on the corner. The walk took us past a row of shops, a good half mile, to the bus. John wasn't happy, so Mam came with us that first day.

St Patrick's school was in the Belgrave area of Leicester on Harrison Road, all old Victorian terraced houses. John screamed and shouted. Then his nose started bleeding, haemorrhaging, and they had to call an ambulance. I thought, *You lucky sod!* Off he went with Mam in the ambulance, leaving me there on my own.

There were about twenty-five of us in the class on my first day at school. The teacher was nice. She gave me a book with a postman on it, a scribbler book. She read the register. Everyone said 'Yes, Miss', or 'Here, Miss.' Then she asked for dinner money. Everyone gave her their 2/6 and she ticked them off. Then she shouted my name.

I went up. 'I haven't got it,' I said.

'Did you forget it?'

'No,' I said, 'I wasn't given any.'

'OK. You bring 2/6 tomorrow,' she said.

'Yes,' I replied, as she wrote a little note.

The rest of the day went well. I played cowboys and Indians, which nearly killed me, with my mates John O'Connor, Christopher

Griffin, Jeremiah Morrissey, and Pete Kavanagh. Then they gave me my dinner. It was beautiful – and pudding.

I went back on the bus, about three miles, to Mowmacre Hill. There was Mammy and Mary! They kept John in hospital to have an operation on his nose. I gave Mam the note.

She went mad. 'Where am I gonna get 2/6? And 2/6 for John? And Mary starting next year? I'll be down there tomorrow,' she told me.

So she came down on the school bus to see Mrs Travis, the headmistress, who looked to me as if she were seventy or eighty, but she couldn't have been.

'I'm on me own with three children,' Mam said to her.

'Leave it to me,' Mrs Travis said, 'I'll speak to the governors.'

There was some kind of discussion among the governors, and lo and behold, they paid for our school dinners – we never paid a penny for school meals in our lives. We were the first to get free school meals; all the other poor kids were close enough to go home for their lunch. Though we would probably have starved without them, we got stick about it as we got older. They cut the serving dishes into eight portions. There'd be eight at a table, and there'd be seconds. There'd be a rush. We'd get, 'No, you haven't paid for yours.' But those meals kept us fed.

The next day I was getting to know a few people, make friends, you know. When I got home that night, John was out of hospital.

'What's that school like?' he said.

'It's alright. You'll like it.'

On the bus the next morning, John was a bit nervous. There was a bit of a kick-off when we arrived, but he went off with the teachers who showed him a bit of affection because he'd been in hospital, and they remembered the drama from a couple of days before. We settled into St Pat's, John in the year above me, both of us in the

Infants playground. It's still there now – two playgrounds, one for the Infants, one for Juniors, with apparatus in both.

It was summertime then. We would come home and have our tea – Swiss roll. Mam would be out cleaning offices; she used to take Mary with her.

St. Patrick's Church

Chapter Five

Our House and Life in General

We'd been in our house for a couple of years. The stairs were on the right after coming through the front door. Upstairs were the much longed-for toilet and bathroom. Next door was Mam's bedroom, then mine and John's. And then the box room. Mary sometimes slept in there, or in Mam's room. Back downstairs was a little hall, then straight into the lounge. We had a settee, a table and chairs, a sideboard and a canary. There was a very old picture of Mam's mam, dad, brother and her sisters on the wall. That was the only thing Mam had left of her family when they were all together. I have no idea how she managed to get it. There were pictures of the Blessed Sacrament and Our Lady. Also, a bottle with a boat inside it that someone had made in Ireland and Nora had brought back. The kitchen had a built-in pantry and two cupboards, a sink, a table, four chairs and the back door. There were no carpets upstairs, on the stairs, or even in the lounge, just rugs. Mam was saving up for lino for the lounge. If you looked out of the lounge window, you could see all the way down the street.

We were all excited. Great news. Nora was getting a house at the bottom of our street. Mam worked for the ex-Lady Mayoress. Her son happened to be on the council and he managed to wangle it with the pushing of papers, whisperings in the right ear, calling in of favours. Because they were pulling St George Street down, he managed to get Nora a house down our street, just around the corner.

It was the same way we got our house. We had a knack for that kind of luck. It wasn't long until we were down there waiting for the big removal truck and Nora, Mack and their dog Lassie to turn up. We helped them with the furniture. It was great to have Nora at the bottom of our street, even just for the food – Nora's cooking. She loved kids and the two things were a lucky mix.

It didn't take Nora and Mack long to settle in. Whenever we could, we were down there helping her. 'Anything I can do, Aunty Nora?'

'Go out and chop me some wood,' or 'Give me a hatchet,' she'd say. Then you'd come in and there would always be a slice of apple pie or something its equal.

About fifty per cent of the estate had to pass our house to get to the shops or the pub, the Tudor Rose, because the bus route ended just round the corner from our house. Most of the lower half of Mowmacre Hill were regulars past our gate. While we were in the garden, just kids playing around, we'd get fireworks thrown at us, abuse shouted at us.

'Fuck off home, Paddy!' We didn't know what they were on about. We didn't know it was because we were Irish.

Nora would never pass the house without coming in. On Saturdays she used to do a bit of shopping at the Co-op round the corner. 'D'ye want to come and help me?' she'd say.

'Yes!' There'd be a treat in it. We'd walk in, she'd put stuff in the basket, stuff in her pockets.

She'd pass me something. 'Eat it.' We'd walk around eating and I'd be as full as anything when I came out. I thought it was normal. I never questioned why Nora put so much of the stuff, tins of salmon and so on, into her pockets. At school we were being taught that stealing was wrong.

I was learning the catechism at the time, getting ready for my First Holy Communion. I couldn't wait. Honourable Christian soldiers marching off to war. I had this vision of us dressed as Roman soldiers – me, John O'Connor, Billy Kilby and the boys. I thought that when I got older I'd get a sword and run those bastard Cannons through because I'd be invincible.

Nora was a great storyteller. She used to tell me the horrors of the Black and Tans back in Ireland when she was a young girl, burning down the houses, burning down the city of Cork.

'Jeekers Neddy, they were mad men, taken from the jails of England and Scotland – murderers, rapists, hand-picked for their hatred of Catholics. The same way they picked the regiment to police Ireland, all from the Protestant Scottish regiments and the like. They'd have men who were just seeing to their own business lined up with guns to their heads, playing roulette.' She would always say 'Jeekers Neddy' and never a 'Jesus, Mary and Joseph' to avoid blaspheming.

She'd send me white with fright.

Nora and Mack were born in West Cork in the 1900s. Like every other man of his generation, Mack became a member of the Old IRA. What exactly Nora's involvement was, she never made clear. Mack was once stopped from coming back to England after one of their return trips because of his involvement with the IRA. It took him a year of arguing his case to get them to let him back in. Another story was that there had been a police raid on their house in London and guns had been found hidden up the chimney. How they got there was not clear, but Nora always had Irish lodgers.

Nora would say, 'When ye get older, ye get off to America, to Montana. All yer millionaire relations are over there.' I used to think, *Where the hell is America?*

Mack was working on the railways at the time, which had been his job in London. He was offered a transfer and that was how they ended up in Leicester. They always missed Ireland, but there was nothing there for them.

The bullying we endured was horrendous. They would get hold of us, me, Mary, and John, and force us to speak 'Irish'. We'd make our way to the shops and that was where they'd get us.

'*Tree-tins-of-turpintine*,' they'd make John say. That's three tins of turpentine, which my mother had sent us to fetch one time.

'Go on, you bogtrotter!'

'Top of the morning to ye,' I'd reply. The Cannons were some of the worst. They were twice our age. Mam would come out shouting if she saw them. Nora wouldn't stand for it, but she wasn't always around.

The summer ended. Autumn and winter came and it was really cold. Icicles hung from wherever they could, and snow banked up, becoming blacker by every passing day. No place was colder than Mowmacre Hill, stuck out on its own, surrounded on three sides by fields. The Stocking Farm estate was on the other side of a green valley.

Our house was freezing all the time, no matter what. The coal fire was only lit at night and that wasn't much. If we ran out of coal, we burned wood. We got into bed buried under blankets and coats.

Then we were up for school, trudging through wind that stung your knees and shook your arms, and air steaming from your mouth like smoke. John had his duffle coat. When he grew out of it, I'd have it. We'd pick up the O'Connors and go on down the hill to the bus.

I took to going to Nora's at night if I could, early in the evening just after the sun went down. Mack would be home then. She'd have a roaring fire and I'd snuggle up on the settee, listen to the radio, or sometimes Mack cuddled up to us, telling us stories.

Then there'd be more just listening to the wireless, all the while with them clearing their throats and spitting into the fire. They were both heavy smokers, smoking Woodbines. It wasn't any sort of Irish tradition or anything. They thought nothing of it.

Lassie, their dog, wasn't the same anymore. She'd become very fat. Nora explained. 'That dirty bitch has gone out and got herself pregnant.' So that's how Lassie was, slow and pregnant.

Pretty soon it'd be time to go home. Nora would go to the pub every night with Mack, dropping us off on the way. We'd settle down, sit and listen to the radio. No telly. Everyone else seemed to have tellies, but we didn't.

Often as not, it'd be, 'C'mon, Timmy, try this on.' Mrs So-and-So had dropped off a bag of clothes – second-hand kids' clothes. Then, 'Oh, that's nice.'

When we headed up to bed, I'd be next to John. Ice would have formed on the inside of the window. It was freezing.

Then it was up, wash your face, downstairs, toast. We huddled round the electric stove, then marched half a mile to the bus stop, climbed into the slightly warmer bus, and off to school.

Chapter Six

Black Sheep, Blind Dogs, and Christmas

The following summer they were starting to gang up on us, except for a loyal handful. The neighbours had fallen out. It was an awful summer. John had been shitting all over the place, in people's gardens, and setting fire to anything that would burn. He had persistent nightmares, screaming the house down. Mam was determined to knock it out of John, so she got him an appointment with a psychiatrist.

When I look back, I realise everyone should have understood. They'd ripped him out of a rural Irish farm on the edge of Cork, where Cork ends before it falls into the sea, and planted him in a council estate in Leicester, nearly as far away as you can get without leaving these islands. No one could understand his Irish brogue, a soft whisper. He missed his grandparents more than he would have missed one of his arms, and he missed the animals on the farm. He couldn't cope with school, didn't want to know. His stay in Ireland was only meant to be temporary, while Mam got herself sorted out. She couldn't cope with the three of us and figure out how to survive and provide for her family on her own.

The worst thing was that we had to go to the Royal Infirmary one day. They told John and me that we were blind as bats. Mam had always needed glasses, so I suppose it should have come as no surprise. I was nearly six and John was seven. Before we knew it, we were given National Health glasses. John wouldn't wear them at all. No way. I can't remember him ever wearing them. I was told, 'Wear them and your eyes will get better.' So that was me with my glasses on – wire things they were. God knows how John managed. He was as blind as me, but he never wore them.

One Sunday morning I got up and went down to Nora's. She was in the kitchen so I went round the back. Nora opened the door. I looked at her and thought, *What are you doing?* Lassie had had her pups and Nora was drowning them in the sink, the little furry things. Their eyes weren't even open.

'Jeekers Neddy, son, give me a hand, Timmy,' she said.

'What d'you want us to do?'

'Wrap 'em in paper.'

So she handed me the dead pups and I wrapped them in newspaper. By the end we had eight little bundles of paper. She took them out to the dustbin and put them in.

I wanted to cry, but I was an honourable Christian soldier and honourable Christian soldiers didn't cry. I just thought, *What d'you do that for?*

Then there was 'Jeekers Neddy,' or 'Get away with ye,' and that was that.

It stayed with me all my life. She couldn't feed them. It was normal back then.

Mary and I were left on our own a lot in the house. Mam couldn't do much about it; she'd just ask her neighbour, Kate Smith, to keep an eye on us. One day Mam flung open the door with John behind her. 'Holy Mary Mother of God, get up them stairs – you're making a right show of me!' she shouted. John shot up the stairs. She was fuming.

'What's up, Mammy?' I asked.

'Never mind what's up. He's made a right show of me in front of that Doctor Carmichael.' Mam had taken him to the psychiatrist about his nightmares, the screaming, the hollering and the shitting. She was out to tame the Wild Colonial Boy. That was what Nora and Mack called him. Nora and Mack were my godparents; I always thought that was why they showed so much favouritism towards me. Mind you, they were sweet with Mary as well.

'You'll never make good of that boy, Kathleen,' Nora would say, referring to John. For the moment the incident with Lassie's pups had left my mind.

When winter set in, we were put to bed every night at five o'clock while Mam went to work as a barmaid. Mam was the perfect employee: she was very jokey and friendly, but never drank. Well, she might have had a drop on St Patrick's Day and at Christmas, but Mam was no drinker. Once she'd gone, we children would soon get up and be playing around. John often wanted a shit. He would either force us to sit at the top of the stairs or, if we wouldn't, we'd lock ourselves in the bedroom. He'd shit into the newspaper and throw it into the fire. That was our night, watching his turd burn on the fire. John was fascinated by fire. He used to get all excited watching the flames. He was never an arsonist; he just liked watching a fire.

Christmas was on its way. We'd get one present each out of Marie's club book next door. When the club book was coming round, we'd pick a present. Mam would start saving up way back in the summer, and store up tins of fruit, and try and make it as best she could.

When Mam was out working and we'd been sent off to bed, we were supposed to kneel down and say our prayers. I did; Mary did. Sometimes we'd pile into one bed and John would tell us stories, like Br'er Rabbit or stories of his life on the farm back in Ireland.

Eventually it was Christmas morning. We had a little tree on the sideboard with a couple of dolls on it, tinsel and a candle. When we woke, we'd be looking for our toys. They'd be on the floor along with a couple of extra toys people had brought round, little stocking-filler presents. It took us about an hour to get bored with them. John would always have something to do with farms, toy animals, tractors. Mary had dolls, and I had soldiers and forts.

One year I climbed up the sideboard. I liked that candle, and lit it. The whole thing went up, burning the ceiling. Mam raced down the stairs. She'd had a late night working in the pub. She ran to the kitchen and back, putting the fire out with a bucket of water. She threw what was left of our Christmas tree out into the garden.

'Jesus, Mary and Joseph! You've wrecked Christmas!' she said.

So, as she was up, she got us dressed in our school uniforms. We all set off to Mass, then came home and had our Christmas dinner. We played with our toys for a bit, followed by a game of Ludo, then it was time for bed. That was that.

New Year came and went. It didn't mean much to us. It wasn't a holiday so people were back at work, though Scottish people we knew would work Christmas Day in order to have New Year's Day off.

Christmastime for John, Tim and Mary

Chapter Seven

Communion

It was the run-up to my First Holy Communion, and I was very excited. The boys were sitting on one side of the church and the girls on the other. We had to go to the priest and tell him our First Confession. I told him a few things like swearing, being cheeky. I learned at an early age not to tell them I'd stolen anything because, otherwise, they'd try and make you put it back or make you repay whatever it was if you'd eaten it. So I used to keep all that a secret and just say nothing.

The big day came and it was a school day. The whole class made their First Communion together. Our church, near St Pat's, was Our Lady's. We were all there; Mam came down with friends. I was in my white shirt, red tie, shorts, and shiny black shoes and socks. We all looked the same, all the boys, and the girls looked fine in their dresses. I was waiting for the host, God's body. You weren't allowed to eat anything and could only drink water until you'd received the host.

I went up, followed the other boys. I took the host in my mouth, the Body of Christ. As I went back to my place, it touched my teeth.

I had this vision of me biting Christ and I burst into tears. It wasn't supposed to touch your teeth. Mam came over.

'I've bitten Jesus.'

'It's alright, He wouldn't have felt it. Swallow,' she said.

Then we went into the church hall and had our Communion breakfast, which was just sandwiches. I'd got over biting Jesus and people were slipping me shillings. I was a soldier now, a Christian soldier. It felt like the biggest day of my life. As we left to go home (it was a short day for us), Mam relieved me of the shillings I had accumulated.

'I'll look after that,' she said.

So there I was, Timothy Joseph O'Sullivan, an honourable Christian soldier.

I started to wise up early. I wondered why we had to sit in the dark at home some nights with the lights off. *Why do we get free school dinners? Free school uniforms? Why are we the only kids on the street that don't go on holiday? Why haven't I got a dad?*

I heard Mam mention that my dad's name was Timothy as well. *Why do we take second-hand clothes off the neighbours?* And food – why did people bake us food and bring it to the house?

Then it hit home. We were fucking dirt poor. We never had many sweets; the only time we had sweets was when somebody called round, mainly Mam's friends from other parts of Leicester. We didn't get any pocket money. You learned a lot from your friends at school.

'What does your dad do?'

'I don't know. I've never seen him.'

'Where is he?'

'I don't know.'

Us kids weren't told anything, but Nora used to say she hadn't much time for my old man.

I started to look at life a bit differently. It wasn't all love and tenderness – it was a shitty old world out there. That was how things were looking. When we questioned Mam about why we never had any pocket money, it'd be, 'Ah, Jesus, I've not got any money. I'm bringing up three children.'

'But everyone else does.'

Out of guilt, I think, she decided on threepence, which was worth about twenty pence, given to us on Saturday mornings. I was seven, nearly eight. The three of us, after the mandatory toast, would pester her. She'd say, 'Go on, go on over to the shops and hold hands and watch the road.' We only had one road to cross, where the bus pulled into the terminus. Off we'd trot. We'd spend twenty minutes working out what we were going to buy. Mind you, you could get a lot for a few pence. Twelve Black Jacks or penny sherbets. Old Bill in the paper shop – he had patience, him and his wife Elsie. Everyone felt sorry for us.

Well, not quite everyone. That was when the taunting really got to me. As I came out of the shop one day, Gaz Wright came running over to me.

'What yer doin' with my top on?'

He punched me in the face and persisted in trying to pull me around and wrench my top off. Eventually he got it off. I couldn't put up much of a fight against him, but I did my best. Mary was crying, John froze, and I lost my sweets. The gang with him soon had them.

'Go on, you bogtrotting bastards – stealing clothes, is it? Gypos. Dirty knackers!'

I went back crying and told Mam what had happened. His mother had given us a bag of clothes – charity for the poor family at the top of the street. I wasn't keen on wearing second-hand clothes, though. I'd sooner have worn John's old cast-offs.

Mam sent me to the shops in a turquoise bathing costume. She insisted I wear it for the neighbours to see.

'Boys don't wear them, Mam.'

'Get it on. I want to see it.'

I had to rush to the shops in this bathing costume at eight years old.

The rag 'n' bone man, Piggott, had a yard not far from our house. When we had completely worn out the second-hand clothes that had been given to us, Mam packed them up into suitcases. Then we'd walk past all the neighbours with these cases.

'Going on holiday are you?' they'd jeer. We'd keep on walking down to Piggott's and drop off the cases full of rags. When we got there, he would weigh them and give Mam money for the clothes.

I think it was about this time, when I was around eight and clothed in other kids' cast-offs, that Mack decided to give me my first job – just helping him out on Saturdays. Mam and I would go down town on the bus together. She'd start her shift at the Rainbow and Dove, a rough Irish pub. Mack was working nearby on a derelict site being used as a temporary car park. He sat in a wooden shed with a heater reading his paper. I was his assistant; I was given a money belt and expected to stay and collected the fees. I felt important. It was a start.

When Mack reckoned I could manage, he would leave me alone to run things as he sloped off for his lunch break. He gave me his cap to wear while he was in the Rainbow and Dove pub. I greeted the drivers as they arrived and asked how long they would be staying in the car park. I had no watch or any way to tell the time, but I had the distinct feeling these lunch breaks were getting longer and longer. After the car park was locked up, we'd both go over to the pub and wait for Mam to finish her shift. My 'pay', apart from a few coppers from drivers when making change, was a pop and crisps, and the Irish lads kept me topped up once Mack had bought the first lot.

One afternoon, a well-dressed guy strolled up to our car park shed, asking for Mack. I simply told the truth. 'He's on his lunch break.' The fellow asked how long he had been gone. I couldn't say, with no way to tell the time. When the man found out Mack was in the pub, Mack lost that job. His lunch break was only supposed to be twenty minutes. Was he taking advantage of me? Sure. But he knew how to boost my confidence, give me a bit of responsibility, plus a bit of a treat in the pub afterwards. But less than two years later, Mack was dead. Tough life, heavy smoker. Maybe he was feeling under par, and that was why those lunch breaks grew longer.

Chapter Eight

Summer

The summer holidays were upon us, and when we returned to St Pat's school in September, we would move up a year. The holiday was nine weeks long and the summer was a proper summer, red hot. There were only a handful of other kids who went to St Pat's on Mowmacre Hill. The rest of the kids went to school on the estate. We were pretty isolated.

In the holidays, all the kids would be in the street. We made some friends. We knew the kids next door, Julie and Elaine. The Murphys were just down the street, with Kathleen, then Billy, who was John's age. The Brooks had moved in two doors from us. They were black, but the parents were a mixture because the mother, Charlotte, was Indian. Mr Brooks was a big fellow. Their two daughters were Betty and Gilda. Mr Brooks used to make kites, which were only about threepence each. We used to fly them, and play chasing them on the street. The Brooks had a dog; there were lots of dogs on the estate, packs of them.

I woke up one morning with a terrible pain in my stomach – I was nearly crying with it. Mam took me to the doctor's, Dr Heffner, who was Irish. We had two doctors, Dr Craig and Dr Heffner, both Irish. Dr Heffner was a smart-looking man who smoked Woodbines. He'd be smoking when you went into his office.

'What can I do for you, Mrs O'Sullivan? What's the matter with Tadhgeen?' Tadhgeen was my name in Gaelic – that was what John used to call me.

'Pain in my stomach,' I managed to say.

Dr Heffner examined me and suspected a grumbling appendix. 'If it gets any worse, you bring him straight back,' he said.

That night I was crying into my pillow, so Mam took me back the next day.

Heffner wasn't in so we saw Dr Craig, who was a man for his whiskey. He was a big, fat, hands-on, ginger-haired fellow. 'I'll have a look at him,' he said, and tickled me.

Even though my stomach was poorly, I giggled.

'Ah, he's just strained his stomach climbing trees or something,' he said dismissively.

We came out. 'I ain't been climbing trees, Mammy. It's killing me.'

She got on the bus with me and we went straight to Accident and Emergency at the Leicester Royal Infirmary. They checked me over, then kept me in. It turned out I did have a grumbling appendix and if I'd gone any longer, it would have burst and it could have killed me. They removed my appendix and I was in hospital for two weeks. I liked it in the children's ward. Mammy would come and see me, always on her own. I don't know who looked after John and Mary.

I soon recovered. I had to go to a convalescent home out in Market Bosworth for another two weeks, a good way out of town. Mam would come and visit me at weekends. It was too much, too far, for her to come more often. The rest of the kids went home at weekends, but somehow I ended up being the only kid there. The nurses would make a right fuss of me at night, let me come and watch telly with them. I'd seen one before at Kate Smith's, but not often. It was brilliant.

After the 'strained muscle' incident, Mam went and smacked Dr Craig round the face after Mass one Sunday.

I was back home and back at school. They all asked me how I was and I showed them my battle scar. It stretched about four inches across my stomach.

'Give us a look at yer scar, Timmy.'

Not long after, Billy Kilby and I ended up fighting. We'd always fought since the first week. We had been caned at just five years old by Miss Travis, the old bird, two on each hand. Never felt them really. This time Mr Perluca, the Polish teacher, broke us up.

'He's hurt my stitches, sir,' I said.

He got hold of Billy Kilby and gave him the hiding of his life – slapped him around and threw him in the cupboard. I felt sorry after that. He was in there, and I was out, free and clear. Our classroom was in the church hall at Our Lady's due to overcrowding. St Pat's school consisted of Irish, Italian, Polish and some English Catholics. They also had the use of classrooms in another school down the road, about a ten-minute walk from St Pat's. At dinner time off we went, all holding hands in twos. We had our dinner and came back. Poor Billy Kilby was still in the cupboard.

When Mr Perluca eventually let him out, he went home and told his mother. The next day she marched into the classroom and whatever kept her from smacking him, I don't know; she was that close. We became great mates after that, me and Billy. I used to go round to his house. His mother looked after us, spoiled us, and our mate Bairdy. All my friends lived in the Belgrave area of Leicester, near St Pat's school.

Chapter Nine

St Pat's School

I will remember the day Peter Baird walked into class, always.

'Peter Michael Baird, miss.'

He always got that 'Michael' bit in. His mam and dad lived in a pub, the Great Northern, in Belgrave Gate. He invited us to his seventh birthday party – me, Mary and John. The pub yard was full of kids. John was tripping people up so he would win the games, the prize being a Kit-Kat bar. Peter's mother gave us a toy each to take home. We had a great time.

In the gang were John O'Connor, Billy Kilby, Paul Hadley, Chris Griffin, and a Dublin kid who was Chris's right-hand man and never far from his side, Jeremiah Morrissey, or Jerry. The Morrisseys were as poor as us, but they had a dad. Jimmy Burke, a rich kid whose family lived out in Birstall, was also one of the gang.

Playtime at St Pat's was time for cowboys and Indians. We would be the US Cavalry. I would draw the cross sabres, the sign of the US Cavalry, on my soldiers' arms, and add TOS: the sign that they were in my gang. We had apparatus in the playground and we would charge around. The girls played skipping and hopscotch. A friendship had grown among the lads. We'd all made our First Confession. We'd all made our First Communion together.

The nurse was there. Normally that meant she'd check us for nits and look at our teeth. Not on this occasion. It was the cough and drop. She'd bring us in three at a time, tell us to drop our trousers and our pants. It was a bit of a shock. She'd put her hands between our legs and ask us to cough.

It came to our turn – me, Billy, and John O'Connor. John was first and he must have got a bit excited. She slapped him round the head and told him to 'Get over in the corner. Control yourself, boy.'

We laughed. She brought him back, tapped his prick with a cold spoon and sent him outside. Then it was me and Billy, trying to stifle the giggles, then we went outside, away from the nurse's slaps. We howled with laughter; Billy was crying with it.

One day in the afternoon, after we'd had our dinner, just the boys from our class were taken into the school hall. We thought they were going to show us a film. The brothers were there, the Christian Brothers, priests who were recruiting. They got you at an early age to head you for the collar. They were showing slides of young would-be priests swimming and playing sports, having a grand old time. I looked at them and thought, *That looks good*. But you needed to be clever to be a priest. We were struggling with Latin. We could manage it, but not to any great extent. I don't think they hooked any catches out of us, but they did push it. The boys and I weren't interested. We wanted to go to America and become cowboys.

Another Saturday, another pocket money day. Off we went to the shop. They were waiting, Steve Patman and his gang. His dad was Sid, the window cleaner, a big guy who ate spiders for bets. Not much happened on Mowmacre Hill that he didn't know about.

Patman came over and started threatening us, 'Paddy' this, 'bogtrotter' that, but this time John gave him such a belt on the side of his head, it sent him flying across the road. His ear split open, and blood was pumping out of it. His gang just stopped and stared. They couldn't believe their eyes. Steve Patman, laid out on the floor – defeated.

'Come on,' John said to me and Mary.

As we walked, they were still standing there open-mouthed. We walked through them. Things changed after that. No more bullying at the shops. We'd still get the Cannons coming up the street, though. They were old enough to drink, and shouted their abuse: 'Hey, glasses.' I had my glasses by this time. They'd throw stuff into the garden, but that was standard. There were no more gangs waiting to pounce on us. It was all 'Hey, Paddy, John L.' That was the nickname John got after that. John L. Sullivan was the world's first heavyweight boxing champion from Boston in America in the 1930s. He'd fought sixty four rounds, bare knuckle. Big John L. Sullivan, that was my brother.

After that incident we went on to be friends with the gang. Steve was a very good footballer and had trials with Manchester United in his early teens. If there was a kick-about, Steve would lend me some boots. He used to call me Paddy Crearan (from Manchester United). In later years he ran a successful taxi business with his dad, Sid.

That was just the confidence John needed. He was sitting on the toilet by then. Still had to have the light on, mind you. Still had his nightmares. Still seeing the psychiatrist, but things had eased. The neighbours had started talking again, Marie and Mrs Hedley. At least John had stopped shitting in their gardens.

Great news. We came home one day in 1963 and there was a television! Big black thing. I don't know where Mam got it. We were the last people on the estate to get one. I now knew what the boys were on about at school when they were talking about *Wooden Tops, Rag, Tag and Bobtail*, and *Andy Pandy*. We loved it. The children's programmes didn't start until four o'clock. We weren't allowed to touch the television, even if Mam wasn't there. If we wanted to change the channel, we'd have to go and find her. Mam loved that telly. There were soap operas; I think Coronation Street had just started. It was fascinating.

We were put to bed early at five o'clock. If Mam wasn't going out, we couldn't watch telly, so John had a crazy idea. He reckoned we could bore three holes through the floorboards, right down through the living room ceiling. I don't know how we didn't hit some wiring and kill ourselves – pure luck really. We didn't bore the holes, though, we used a red-hot poker to burn through the wood and through the ceiling. Sure enough, three holes were made, but we still couldn't see the telly. We'd have needed a periscope to manage that, but we could hear it.

Now we had our own telly, John had a bit of street cred on the estate, and the bullying had eased. Pocket money had risen to sixpence. Things were looking up.

Cornflakes was another good sign. John would have toast as well. You could never fill that lad up. He was getting bigger than ever and he looked a right prat in his short pants. He was forever outgrowing his clothes; his school uniform would never last him the year – he'd get through two, sometimes three. They'd only give you one uniform, so you wore the same clothes all week. They were washed and we were bathed on Sunday nights, the three of us.

Mam was doing well with her cleaning job in the daytime and the pubs at night. She didn't have to pay for babysitters. She always worked in Irish bars, for Irish couples who would pay her less than the going rate because it was in cash and the authorities wouldn't find out. She was getting National Assistance to help bring us up, along with her Family Allowance. We used to go and collect it. It was about ten shillings, and it was all we had.

Billy O'Connor came round to fit a carpet. It was second-hand, but who cared? We had a stair carpet! There was lino in the lounge now and tiles in the kitchen, and a big rug in the hallway which was the first thing you saw when you opened the door. It was still hard floorboards upstairs, with just a few rugs, but things were getting better.

Any odd job around the house, Billy O'Connor would do it. He was a lovely, God-fearing man, who never drank, never smoked, just bred kids. By this time there were five of them. Bridget was John's age, Marian was mine. Then there was Brendan, a bit of a gap, and then the twins. Mam's best friend was their mother, Sheila. They were great friends for years, and Billy was dead helpful.

Then Billy's father died in Limerick. Billy was the last one, the youngest, to carry on the farm, so he had to go back. It was a sad day when the O'Connors left for Ireland. They packed up everything into the removal van, we waved goodbye, and they were gone. Sheila cried and Mam missed her. We missed the girls.

Going to school then became a different ball game. With Mam working late in the pubs, she didn't fancy the walk. We were old enough, aged seven, eight and nine. There were exactly eleven months between me and John and between me and Mary.

One night Mam reminded us that the next day was St Patrick's Day, the patron saint of Ireland, our feast. We always loved St Patrick's Day – everyone was always in a good mood.

We woke up and put on our little badges, the green rosettes. We had two, and pinned one on our sock and one on our breast pocket. Off we went, full of excitement, knowing it was going to be a special day at school. We had two roads to cross. There was a big green area dividing the two estates and I ran across the road. Next thing I knew, I was waking up on the road. Apparently I'd been knocked over by a moped or a motorbike. I was knocked out and sent flying. Some parents came running over and someone fetched my Mam. She came down and I seemed alright when I came round, so she took me to school. She had plans to go to Mass, probably, then work.

I didn't feel right at school. I came home and went to bed early, but I woke up in the middle of the night with this conviction that John was chasing me, and was going to kill me. I ran out into the street. It seemed pitch black. I went down to Nora's, but she wasn't in. She and Mack would still be out celebrating. I went to Kate Smith's and ended up sitting in her sitting room watching the telly until Mam came home. Kate was another neighbour who liked gossiping with Mam. Kate and Marie never got on.

That was my St Patrick's Day. I never did go to hospital.

That summer, Nora and Mack went on their annual return trip to Ireland. This time they took Mary so she could go and see the grandparents in West Cork. Nora was from Skibbereen, like my Mam, about twenty-five miles from the farm. Then they went on to Puck Fair in Kerry. The Puck Fair was a tradition that stretched back into the mists of time. Up in Tralee, the pubs would stay open for three days and nights. Mam and Bridget used to go with them in the early days. Mam and Bridget weren't drinkers, but they used to have to spend days in the pub singing old rebel songs. Nora and Mack would get drunk. They loved the drink, the pair of them.

So off Mary went with them and I was jealous; I didn't get to go. They could handle Mary. Nora and Mack entered Mary into the Rose of Tralee junior beauty pageant and she won, since she had that long ginger hair. She had a great time.

When she got home, we saw she had scabs all over her. They said it was due to the water. For the next few years, her nickname was 'Scabby'. John's was 'Psycho', and mine was 'Four Eyes' because of the glasses I dutifully wore.

Nora would always bring us back something from her Irish holidays. Everything in Ireland was so cheap back then.

School photograph of Timothy Joseph Patrick O'Sullivan taken at St. Patrick's School, Harrison Road, Leicester

St. Patrick's School

*School photograph mid 1960's
Tim is stood middle row far right*

Chapter Ten

The Den

It was turning towards autumn. I was given the chore of cleaning out Joey, the canary. I liked doing that – I'd let him fly around. The cage was getting a bit shabby, and the glass on the sides was broken. I had to change his water, put fresh sandpaper in the bottom, and clean his mirror. Joey never chirped much. I don't know why we bothered, but we loved him. He was our pet.

On our Christmas holidays, John decided to explore what was the other side of the gap in the landing, up on the ceiling. He got up there and shouted for us to join him. We pulled each other up into a big black attic. Cold, it was. That was our secret den. We soon decided to make our den more homely.

On Sundays we went to church at night. There were two morning Masses, 8.30 and 10.30, then 6.30 on Sunday night. We tended to go to that because it meant we could have all day playing. Catholics were allowed to eat before Holy Communion now since the rules were eased and modernised. The Holy Ghost was changed to the Holy Spirit and such like. In the church there were small candles.

We got up and pretended to light one for the dead and filled our pockets with them, hoarding them for our den.

The next weekend we went up there with our candles and some books that people had given to Mam. Mary pretended to be a secretary. We used to light a little fire, and we hid everything up in the attic. Mam used to paste us with the spatula, with coat hangers, or a rolling pin if we'd done something wrong. They all ended up in the attic.

We played around up there for months. We always put it back nice, and cleaned when our dirty handprints were left on the hatch. One day I went down to get some water and heard an almighty crash. I ran into the hall and saw John's legs hanging from the rafters. The plaster he'd knocked loose had come down. He was dangling from the rafters and he spotted that the plaster had hit the beautiful big jug and bowl sitting on the landing windowsill. That jug and bowl were the best things we had in our house. Mam kept them on the landing window so people could see them as they walked past.

'Jesus, Tadhgeen, get hold of that!' he yelled.

I rushed to the bottom of the stairs. The jug was bouncing down, one step at a time, boing, boing, boing. Up it went, and I missed it. It smashed to smithereens at my feet. *What are we going to do now?* The plaster was everywhere – and burnt papers, the evidence of our lighting fires. We cleaned up the papers.

We put the telly on; Mam had relaxed the rules about us touching it. Programmes were on a bit more often too. At the weekends there was always something to watch.

Mam came home at three o'clock, after work. 'Jesus Christ Almighty, what's happened?'

'We were playing nice and quiet, or what we thought was quiet, Mam, then that nosey Marie from next door came round, knocked on the front door and told us to be quiet, and as she went out she slammed the door and the ceiling came in and hit the bowl and smashed it,' I blurted out, and the others all joined in. Believe it or not, that excuse lasted. Mam had fallen out with Marie again, over us. They weren't talking, so she actually believed us, which was amazing. Until a few days later, when the council man came round to put the new ceiling in. He was up in the attic and found the remaining burnt papers and our den. We got the hiding of our lives when we got home from school; beat us to a pulp, she did. The council threatened to throw us out of the house for criminal damage.

We gave the attic a rest for a bit. It wasn't long though before we were back up there, though, only this time we were a lot more careful.

I found a stray cat. We knew all the neighbours' pets, but we didn't recognise this one. We gave it what we had left in the house, dry bread and water. I left it downstairs while we went up to play in our den. When I came back down, I noticed Joey's cage had been knocked over. I shouted for John and Mary and we searched for Joey. I pulled back the curtain under the sink. That was where that bastard cat was, halfway through eating Joey. I screamed at it, went to the cutlery drawer for knives and forks to throw at it. I got hold of it, bashed it about, opened the door and threw the half-dead animal over into Marie's garden. Luckily, the fork had fallen out of it and landed in the roses. I was crying my eyes out. I retrieved Joey, put him in a plastic bag, went out and buried him in the garden.

When Mam came home we told her the truth. 'Cat got in and ate Joey,' I said.

'Don't worry, we'll get another one off Jimmy Regan,' she said.

He was a relation of Nora's who lived on Stocking Farm. He dealt in budgies. True to her word, we had another one within a week. We called him Joey too, but he didn't reign long. I went to bed one night and gave him a bit of toast on my way up. I came down in the morning and found him dead as a dodo, with a big lump of toast stuck in his neck. I buried him next to our original Joey. Two Joeys in the garden. No more canaries. No more budgies.

Chapter Eleven

The Pub and Lewis's

After all the trouble with the den, Mam decided she'd take us to work with her. She worked in the Black Lion in Humberstone Gate. Mary was the gaffer, and she had a husband. Mam would send us to the pictures while she worked. In the summer, we could sit in the backyard. All the Irish fellas came in.

'Jesus, are ye Kathleen's children? I knew yer father.'

'Did ye? What was he like?'

'A good man, hard-working man. A fine fighter.'

They got to know us and always slipped us a few pence. The drunker they were, the more you'd get. We'd enjoy it.

One of John's presents that year was a punchbag. It was called Freddie Mills. The punchbag bit was his face. John made up a guy (for Guy Fawkes) with Freddy for his face. We went to town, outside the Black Lion.

'Penny for the guy!'

We made a fortune. Mam took it all off us and gave us back a shilling.

When we went off to the pictures, Mam would walk us up there. There were plenty to choose from in town. When we came back to the pub after the film, Mam's shift would be nearly over. The pub shut about two thirty, and we'd go home.

On Saturdays, before the pictures, we'd go to Lewis's. Lewis's was a big four-storey department store in the centre of Leicester. You could get a bag of broken biscuits each for a tanner. Then we'd go and look at the toy department, upstairs at the back. They had every toy. It was a child's dream.

'What do ye want for Christmas?' John asked.

'I'd like that,' I said.

'I'll get it yer.'

We had these big duffle coats. It was a piece of cake. You'd just pick it up, look at it, drop it in your big sleeve, and put your hand in your pocket. We were getting very good at it. We had another den at the pub, round the back. When our pockets were full, we'd stash all our stuff there, toy trucks, all sorts. It was where all the market traders dumped their old fruit and vegetables. That was also a spot we liked to root through. We'd find stuff to eat – I found a mackerel there once. We told Mam we'd fished it ourselves and took it home for dinner. Mam liked a bit of mackerel.

So we were master thieves. I was ten, John was eleven, and Mary was nine. Mam would ask, 'Where'd ye get all these toys?'

'Mrs Baird,' we'd say. That was Peter's mum, the one that loved us, felt sorry for us. So Mam was happy we had the toys. We took them out of their wrappings and pretended they were second-hand.

Christmas was coming, so we headed back to Lewis's. We were going to have a good Christmas that year. We were on our third trip and had already stashed a load. I went for some balloons to decorate the house. I felt a hand on me, roughly grabbing me. I turned around. There he was, a big military type, all angular faced and grey haired.

'Come with me, young man.'

John and Mary weren't anywhere to be seen. The guy was massive and I was scared. He took me into the office where a couple of secretaries were sitting. My name? I told him. Address? I told him. 'You took the balloons?' I showed them. Then I started crying.

'Right, we'll be reporting you to the police. Now, off you go.'

As I put my hand on the door handle to leave, he said, 'Hang on a minute – let's have a look in your pockets.' He must have caught sight of something. When he emptied them out, he realised this wasn't some innocent from a sweet shop. There were transport tankers, loads of stuff. This really was a matter for the police.

He got on the phone. About an hour later, the police arrived. They took me out and put me into the back of their van, and headed off to Charles Street police station. I sat there in a gloomy Victorian building, scared stiff. Crying wasn't going to help. All I had on me was threepence pocket money. Threepence to get me home.

'Right, Timothy, we'll be coming to see your mum, so I suggest you tell her what you've been up to.'

'I will do, Sergeant.'

'Your name's in the Big Black Book now.'

He wrote something in an enormous old book. They had all the toys as evidence, put away in a cupboard. I couldn't wait to get out of that place.

When I was caught, they asked me who I was with, and I told the store detective about my brother and sister. 'They're thievin' an' all, sir.' I thought, well, if I'm in the shit, I'll have that pair in with me. He went out and had a look for them, but couldn't find them.

The police were big in those days. He was a giant and I was terrified. They walked me out, down the stairs, one on each side, leading me out. Shock tactics. They worked.

When I finally made it home, they were there – John and Mary sitting in front of the telly, watching the football results and the wrestling.

'Where ye been?' Mam said.

'I got lost.'

She went off to the kitchen – it was tea and cakes on Saturdays.

'What happened?' John whispered.

'They nicked me.'

'Are ye gonna tell Mammy?'

'No, leave it.'

I was glad to get into bed that night. It had been a hectic day, the twentieth of December, 1964.

We stayed out of Lewis's – I was banned – and the den contained loads already. But the market traders must have found our stash. A few days later, a knock on the door came early evening.

'Mrs O'Sullivan, we've come about Timothy O'Sullivan.'

'I've not seen him in years.'

There was a pause, eye contact between the officers, confusion.

'Which Timothy are ye referring to?' she asked.

'Timothy O'Sullivan, ten years of age.'

'I thought ye were on about my husband.'

Two CID plain-clothes coppers came in.

'Didn't he tell you he was caught shoplifting at Lewis's?'

'No.'

I didn't get a chance to reply. Her hand came up and hit me straight in the face. I shot across the room. They were happy with that, the coppers, and they left. I was given another few belts, then sent upstairs.

In the morning, I thought that was that. They couldn't take you to court under the age of ten. That was the end of my shoplifting days, and John and Mary's as well, but Mam went on about it for days.

'Jesus, Mary and Joseph! A thief in the house! Don't ye go telling no one.'

I was thinking, *She doesn't know that Nora's nicking stuff all the time. No, I won't bring her into this to ease my guilt.*

That Christmas Day after Mass, there was a knock on the door. Mrs Sheppard worked for the WRVS, thbe Women's Royal Voluntary Service. She had a box of toys for us, all donated. We would soon get to know Mrs Sheppard, who was a lovely woman. Holidays would be on offer. *What's a holiday?* We had yet to find out.

Everyone in Leicester went on holiday in the July Fortnight, the first two weeks of July. The streets emptied. There would just be the old people left and us. We'd be the only ones that never went away. Even the poorer families managed to get a week away in Skegness in a caravan. We didn't.

Not until Mrs Sheppard came along. She organised for us to go and stay with families by the seaside, sometimes together, sometimes at different times, but not with the same families. We only went about three times.

One time, Mary was staying with a family in Cleethorpes and John and I were staying with a Doctor Chandler and his family. It was a nice posh house. They were rich and had their own car, and they had a daughter a bit younger than me. We used to go out, driving along the seaside and have picnics. They took us to the pictures. Their daughter had never done a bad thing in her life until we turned up.

We were up in bed; she was in her own room. We went into her parents' bedroom to see what we could discover. We found a huge box of chocolates in the shape of a heart. It was three foot by two foot. Luckily, it wasn't wrapped up. It had been opened at some point, but only a handful of chocolates were missing. Well, it was bingo! *That'll do nicely.* We stuffed ourselves until we couldn't eat any more. Of course we had to force them down the daughter's throat too, so she'd be as guilty as us. We thought we'd be long gone by the time they missed them – they'd been put on top of the wardrobe. Little did we know.

It wasn't long before Dr Chandler called me and John and the daughter down to the dining room. The chocolates were on the table. *Ah, here we go.* He explained that those chocolates were bought for them on their wedding day and, every year on their anniversary, Doctor and Mrs Chandler would open the box and have one each. That was why only a handful were missing. He was cross, but I knew we weren't going to get a kicking out of him. He was properly brought up, educated – he was a doctor. His wife was crying her eyes out. What was left in the box lasted them another three years. They were the nasty ones we bit and put back. The daughter was crying too, so we pretended to. We were grounded. Grounded from what? We were living in heaven, in a beautiful house and garden. 'No pictures this weekend.' Ah well, we could live with that.

It was time to go home. We left. They kissed us and said they'd keep in touch. True to their word, every Christmas the presents would arrive. They emigrated not long after, but they still sent us gifts all the way from Canada.

Chapter Twelve

Holidays

The side garden was full of potatoes and cabbage. On Saturdays, we'd get ready to go for a walk in the fields. We'd pack up a picnic of a bottle of pop and bread and jam. It was just the three of us – me, John and Mary.

John could have been back on the farm in Ireland. He loved the fields, and he'd think nothing of going up and stroking the animals. We'd walk for hours and one time we came across some horses, so the long fella decided to have a ride. He told me and Mary to cup our hands and give him a lift up. We joined our hands together and he got up. The horse didn't like it. It turned around, grabbed my back, sort of sucking, and then it bit me. I screamed like a piglet. At that, the horse bolted and took off with John riding bareback, tearing away like John Wayne in a Western. It threw him off, but John thought it was great. I didn't think much to it at all.

We headed home with my back bleeding. It wasn't that bad, but it felt worse. I made a big fuss. I was covered in cow shit, filthy.

When we got home, Mam was there. 'Get into the bath.'

She never reared up when we came home filthy. So into the bath I went.

We used to have a bath every Sunday, all three of us. But as we were getting a bit older, Mary wasn't allowed to join us. It was just me and Longshanks, and soap. We even washed our hair with soap. It was a great feeling coming out of the bath spotless – it was only once a week. We had an immersion heater by then. Before that Mam had to put the fire on and warm the water. John would always pass comment on my dick. It wasn't so much that mine was small, it was that his was so big. It was like a baby's arm, but then everything about John was big. We'd then get dry and sit downstairs. The fire would be on. Mam would get her hair grip out, to get the wax out of our ears. He'd be screaming like a banshee again.

When she cut his toenails, you'd think she was cutting his feet off. We'd howl with laughter, me and Mary. Sometimes we'd have to listen to *Sing Something Simple* on the radio. Sunday nights were such depressing times.

Sometimes we'd play in the garden with the kids next door. 'Shall we play doctors and nurses?' It doesn't take much imagination to figure out what that was about – a spot of useful exploration. I went into the shed with Elaine. I explored her body, she checked out mine.

One night Marie came charging round. 'Kathleen, look what I've found on Elaine's knickers!'

John, Mary and I were sitting on the sofa. It was a big black handprint.

'It's that savage son of yours!'

'Don't you call my son a savage!'

I was giggling like hell.

'God knows what he's been doing!'

Mam grabbed the rolling pin. John jumped up and ran behind the telly. She wouldn't dare go anywhere near that. Then he ran around the settee, with me and Mary giggling, and Mam still chasing him.

'Stop him!'

Obediently, a foot went out – most probably mine. John went flying. Mam got hold of him and gave him a beating, then went out to the kitchen to calm down. It would soon be time for her to start her shift.

'You fucking wait, Glasses,' John hissed, 'till Mam's gone out.'

That meant I was going to get a kicking. It explained why the rolling pin went up into the attic. I didn't feel any guilt about it. It was my handprint on her knickers, I knew that.

I'd found myself a nice little earner on Saturdays. There was an old couple in the flats at the bottom of the street. The flats were three storeys high, full of old people. Some of them were housebound and might have been living up two flights of stairs. On the ground floor of the middle block lived the Nice Lady. My duties were to pick up her books and take them over to the library on Stocking Farm. I'd ask the librarian for five similar books. Off I would go. The librarian was typical, a bony woman with glasses poised on the end of her nose. She looked as if she'd never been with a man in her life. She didn't select any more books, just showed me the correct aisle. If she put three back, I'd get three more out. I'd flick through and pick three at random. It was a trek across the valley, but worth 2/6, which was a lot of money. Combined with my pocket money, I had three shillings a week. I thought, *Fuck those second-hand clothes. I'm going to save up.* That went on for a long time. I reckon it was the first sign of my fledgling business acumen.

Things were changing. When Sundays came along, Mam was no longer going to church. She reckoned her back was playing her up. The priest would come to look in on her and bring her Communion. Sunday mornings we'd all be up, dressed smartly in our school uniforms, and off we'd head to church. Sometimes Nora and Mack would go. We'd make our own way there, about a mile, and a mile back. We could walk it now that the new St Pat's had opened. We'd cut through over the valley, through the Stocking Farm, and over the hill.

A new priest had arrived, Father O'Sullivan. He took to us – same name – poor kids with no dad. We knew we couldn't skip going to Mass. The two churches in St Pat's school catchment were Our Lady's and St Patrick's. The teachers that went to St Patrick's knew which children to look out for and checked if they went to Communion. If you didn't, they'd want to know why.

There was one time I had a problem as we got ready for Mass. My shoe had a hole in it. 'Mam, I can't wear them.' You had to kneel down for Communion and everyone would see it.

'Don't worry, I'll fix it.'

She cut some cardboard from the cornflakes packet and put it in my shoe. It wasn't the answer I was looking for, but there was nothing else I could do. Sure enough, while I was kneeling down trying not to bite Jesus, I heard giggling behind me. It turned out Mam had cut the eye of the cock on the packet and it was right where the hole was, so all the people could see was the cock's eyes peering out from the hole in my shoe.

Saturdays meant Confession, but not every Saturday. The three of us would dutifully be there, but never mention stealing, of course.

Mass would be a laugh. We used to be bored stiff. To fill the time, we'd try and spot kids in the Fat Nit Gang, or look out for the red-headed Dr Craig and his family. After that appendix saga, when Mam had smacked him straight in the face, just the sight of him would set us off. We'd giggle, then John would lean over, pull Mary's hair, and set her off again.

Some of the Mass was in Latin and it seemed to go on for ages. It was only fifty minutes, but it felt like two hours. Eventually they modernised the service, changed it into English, and women no longer needed to cover their heads. I always thought they changed the Holy Ghost to the Holy Spirit so it wouldn't scare the children. Anyway, we'd escape at last and couldn't wait to get home. It wasn't so bad in the summer.

We never seemed to pay attention to the sermons, but I remember my aunt Bridget found one priest so frightening, she used to be scared stiff and had been known to be overcome and faint. Strange that I can't recall ever being terrified by a sermon or any particular priest; I might have quite enjoyed the excitement.

One year, as Christmas was approaching, John had an idea. He came out knocking on doors with us. 'We're collecting toys for the orphans, for St Patrick's.'

'Are yer?' Could you come back next week?'

There were a few Catholics on Stocking Farm, but they stayed well clear of us. We didn't have any friends over there. We remembered which houses told us to return, and we'd go back and collect the toys. A lot of them were broken, but it was better than nothing. Mary had the dolls, John chose the animals and I'd have the soldiers and forts. It worked for a while, but we were soon fed up with it and stopped.

On one memorable day at school, we were all at assembly and Mrs Travis, the headmistress, was up front addressing us. She was no longer in her first youth and that day she was clearly very upset. In my humble opinion, she was on her last legs. She began by making an announcement. 'I have some news. Anthony Brennan, Sean Brennan and David Brennan, please come forward.'

The three brothers, nice lads they were, had been caught robbing the old woman who ran the sweet shop next to St Pat's. Mrs Travis showed them up blind and caned them in front of everyone. I felt sorry for the Brennans, but at least I realised we weren't the only thieves in the school.

Not long after that, Mrs Travis retired. The new man on the block was a Mr Brennan, funnily enough. He was a younger man, in his forties, big and powerful. He brought the modern approach to teaching to St Pat's. Teachers started negotiating with pupils, not simply dictating and getting all their own way. There was an arrogance and even cruelty in children when judging their teachers. I always felt Mrs Travis didn't know what day it was half the time. I thought she was just an old biddy. She was probably worn down and frazzled by stress. Mr Brennan was young, fit and wanted to do things. He was strict, very strict.

Chapter Thirteen

Home and Mablethorpe

Mam and Marie still weren't speaking over the knickers incident. Elaine stayed out of the way for a while. They weren't allowed to come near us.

My birthday, 8 July, was fast approaching and John and Mary chose their toys. They would get their toys on my birthday because mine was the first one in the year. When it was their birthdays, they'd get nothing. Mam said it was fair because everyone had something, so there'd be no arguing. By the time July ended, their toys would be broken. We never had a party, not one of us, ever. We went to plenty of other kids' parties, but we never had one. I suppose that ground into us the fact that we were poor.

Mam would be roaring at night about money, debt and the rent. 'They're gonna throw us out the house,' she'd be going. It would get on our nerves. Sometimes we used to think it was our fault. 'If I'd put you in care, I wouldn't have had this.'

The threats became reality one day. On Saturday a big van landed outside our house. Bailiffs got out, strode down the path, and knocked on the door. They pulled out their papers and started taking our furniture, putting it in the garden. *That's when you know if you've got friends.* The whole street and half the estate were out. Word soon got round – laughing and jeering they were. I'd never felt so shown up in all my life; Mam was raring up. The crowd, our neighbours, all stood round on the pavement. There was a big commotion.

'Hey, Paddy, yer being slung out!'

That was all I needed, fucking Cannon, the one with his two brothers in prison for burglary. That big mutton-headed bastard. I didn't see much of him. He was, as I've said, old enough to drink. He'd just fire the odd bit of abuse on the way to the bus, or on his way to the Tudor Rose, or any Friday, Saturday and Sunday if we happened to be in the garden.

So they were carting out the furniture and they still had a bit to do when a car pulled up. Who jumped out? Father O'Sullivan.

He opened the gate, rushed down the path and demanded to see who was in charge. It was some typical Leicester guy, flat cap, with a fag sticking out of his mouth. Father looked at the paperwork and took what was owing out of his own pocket. 'Now, by God, you take every stick of that furniture back inside and put it back where you found it.'

Saved by the bell, or saved by the priest. We were back in our house. Where would we have gone? Mack was ill, sleeping downstairs. We couldn't really have put upon Mack and Nora. We'd been panicking. We would have had to go into care. Mam would have moved in with Nora. God knows, the thought of that terrified us.

Thank heavens, we were back. We saw those so-called friends of ours in a different light. The only people who'd shown any consideration were the Murphys down the road. They helped us put the stuff back. They walked it in the door and put it where they felt it fit.

We'd beaten the bailiffs. We'd beaten the petitions. There'd been two attempts by the council to have us thrown out for unruly behaviour, mainly John's. The only reason we knew about it was that the Murphys told us. They wouldn't sign the petition.

Life went back to normal. Sundays down to Mass, back home for boiled bacon and cabbage. It was nice, about the only time we had dinner as a family. The school kept us fed. Mam was out a lot more because she'd taken to gambling now, horses or bingo. We'd have a packet of biscuits and a Swiss roll to divide between us. On Sundays there were piles of spuds, a bacon hock, or depending on whether we were in luck, a bacon joint. Most of the time it was bacon hock, a pig's foot. It was tasty and we'd drink the cabbage juice. We each had our place at the table. John had his green plastic plate and cup, Mary had the red one, and I had the blue. In the kitchen there was a stove, a cupboard and a built-in pantry, which now had a lock on it. The lock was put on after one Christmas when we went to the tins of fruit Mam was stocking up, bored holes in them, and drank all the juice. Mam had become a laughing stock when folks came round and saw what we'd done. She tried to keep order by putting on the padlock, but it wasn't long before we learned to pick it. That was just one more thing that went unnoticed. She couldn't fathom where all the food was going.

Mrs Sheppard came through. She was still there every Christmas, and she'd pop in to keep an eye on us. One day when we came back from school, John was told he was going on holiday to Mablethorpe Children's Home. Mmm, that sounded good. Off John went. Mam gave him five shillings to last a fortnight. It soon flew by. John never mentioned much, just that someone called Archibald Hempwhistle was there.

The next year, it was my turn. Mam took me down to Holy Bones. A lot of kids were there with their parents. God, I thought I was poor! This mob were all from Saffron Lane and Braunstone. The buses pulled up. There were tears. I didn't want to go, but I waved goodbye. Mam gave me five shillings in my hand and off I went to Mablethorpe.

We drove up a hill. There was a big white building perched on the top. It was paid for by the hosiery factory owners in Leicester for the workers' children, the poor. And they all were poor, apparently. When we stepped off the buses, it was girls to the left, boys to the right. Then it became military.

'Line up, you scraggy lot.'

We lined up. In we went, one by one. I didn't like it at all, nor did the others. There were some lairy bastards on the bus, but they soon shut up when we landed there.

'This is Matron So-and-So, this is Uncle Ted, Uncle Morris.'

I didn't have an Uncle Ted or an Uncle Morris. *You're no uncle of mine.*

The first night the boys all lined up. We slept in dormitories with a bathroom at the end. Uncle Ted dipped our heads one by one in some stuff in the sink. I later found out it was nit killer, so it stank.

On with our pyjamas. We never had pyjamas at home – Mam had had to go and buy some for John last year. Well, of course, I had those ones. They'd never been touched since. Into bed. I didn't like it. You could hear crying: 'I want me mam.' I felt the same way.

There were a couple of lessons in the morning, which seemed a little odd for a holiday, followed by dinner time. We lined up to go into the big dining room. We hardly ever saw the girls. In the afternoon, it was down to the beach – the great white building actually backed onto the beach. We played boring cricket. No, I didn't like it.

Then one day, Uncle Ted said, 'Right, everyone down to the beach! Not you, O'Sullivan. I want you to help me in the ironing cupboard.'

I thought, *What's his game?* We got in. He shut the door, and said, 'You've been circumcised.'

'Yeah.'

'I'd like to take a look at that.'

I told him, 'You get fucked!' Out I went. He shouted after me, but I just carried on running until I found the rest of the kids on the beach. That dirty bastard never came near me again.

The Lord Mayor of Lincoln came to visit one day. We were in the dining room, and we all sang 'A Bicycle Made for Two' for him. We were all given a shilling each, which was handy. Every two or three days they marched us down to the shops near the beach. You could spend your money on toffee apples, but I couldn't wait to get home. I wrote to my mam, two letters, as best as I could. I couldn't spell 'Leicester', so they ended up being battered around London. London had an LE postcode, London East. The letters finally did arrive, about a month after I had returned.

When I went back to school, all the lads were asking, 'What was it like? Bet it was great!'

'No, it weren't. And how come none of you lot have gone?'

We were the only ones out of St Pat's to go. Every time we went by Holy Bones for years, I'd see the kids lined up. I'd be thinking, I wonder if that bastard Uncle Ted is still there. There they'd be, waiting, all excited.

Chapter Fourteen

John's Leaving

John's last year at St Pat's was 1963. The Beatles were everywhere – it was rock 'n' roll, the Swinging Sixties. Mack used to cut our hair, but since he'd been ill, we went across the road to fireman Frank Franklin instead. He used to come in and put a basin over your head. John wasn't having any of that short back and sides, not since this new era had come in.

At school, Mr Brennan had a mission about me and John, about our hair. Mam had to pay Franklin. If money was short, our hair grew. John then refused to have his hair cut. Mr Brennan would be forever on to us.

'Get your hair cut.'

'Can't afford it.'

'I will personally take you to a barber's and pay for you to have a haircut.'

Which he did.

In John's last year, he used to have our class in stitches. Friday afternoon was sports day. The boys would all come out in their football kit, including boots. We didn't have any boots. All the girls went out to play rounders. So, unable to play, John was sent into our class. He'd get up and tell stories, which the teacher allowed.

Usually they were stories about his adventures on the farm. Even the teacher used to laugh. He'd throw in sound effects too. If he was describing a fart, he'd toss in a great big *thrrrup* for good measure. He had the class in hysterics.

At last, it was time for the summer holidays, our last day – a sad day really. Half of John's class were going to English Martyrs, the other half to Corpus Christi. This meant the guys you had spent your childhood with, and even the girls, you'd probably not see again for years, if you ever did.

We came home. The bus stopped outside the Tudor Rose where we expected the jeering. At ten years old, John must have been five feet tall and was still in his school uniform short pants. All the kids on the estate went to Mowmacre Hill and didn't have to wear uniforms. We had to wear a grey shirt, green and gold tie, short pants, grey jumper and black shorts. That combination really made us stand out.

Eight weeks' holiday stretched out ahead of us. Mam's back had gone completely by then. We had to bring her bed downstairs. Nora had to come up and do the shopping and cook. She took our clothes away and washed and ironed them. She made an art out of ironing and starching.

For those two months we ran riot. That summer was a real scorcher. For the first two weeks of July, Leicester's July Fortnight, the estate emptied. We were left on our own again. We'd go to the pictures a lot. Then everyone came back. We used to get through about ten sticks of rock each. Maybe they were from Nora, from her annual trip back to Ireland. With Mam still laid up, and Nora coming in when she could, we were left to wrestle with the lock on the pantry ourselves if we wanted anything extra to eat.

John's Leaving

Now that we were getting older, we could travel further on the estate. We'd all end up in the fields. Someone would bring an old car tyre and someone else a rope, and we'd rig up a swing. It only took a handful of nails up the trunk to help us climb high enough to get into the swing. Somehow we requisitioned a few bales of hay, and set them out to jump off and land in. When the excitement of that wore off, we became a little more daring. I have a vague memory that this might have been John's idea, but we set fire to the hay and would try to swing over it.

By this time there were more kids in the gang – Brian Oliver, for one, whose family lived off Border Drive. Brian was going to be at secondary school with me. Stewart and Alan Warner were two more. They lived next door to the Olivers. Their neighbours were the Wheeler boys who also joined in. Some of the lads had started smoking. We were toying with it. We couldn't afford them, at any rate. I only had three shillings a week and cigarettes cost two shillings, but you could get five for just under a shilling. We were all well under age, but as long as the money was right, no one seemed too fussed.

We'd scramble back, the dirt of the day stuck to our bodies with the sweat of the summer heat. Nora would be there waiting and getting our tea on.

That wasn't my only pastime. Out the back of our house, I was playing doctors and nurses with Elaine again. She was getting to be a terror. She started smoking. Mam didn't smoke, but Nora did. We used to steal her Woodbines, just take one cigarette. Only one, and you wouldn't smoke it all at once. Smoke it, clip it. You might light the same cigarette five times.

Elaine was put into a home for stealing from her mother. That was a bit drastic, I thought, when you tallied up all the crimes that John, Mary and I pulled off. On that basis, we would have been hung. Marie was like that. Apparently, she'd had a daughter when she was much younger that Marie's mother adopted, Cheryl, nicknamed Sherry. Marie was brutal. Curiously, the husband – her second husband, in fact – was a nice, placid fellow. Takes all kinds.

Chapter Fifteen

Back to School

Sure enough, the holidays soon came to an end. That last week Mam had us back down to John Cheatle's for our free school uniforms. John was getting his new English Martyrs kit. He went to put his shoes on. Mam had had enough of his outgrowing them. He was already a size seven or eight.

'Give him a size ten. I want to get at least another year out of them,' she said.

He looked pretty dandy in his long trousers and his 'Herman' boots. They ended up calling him 'Herman' at English Martyrs, after Herman Munster from *The Munsters* telly show. I had my new St Pat's uniform, a crispy new shirt and a blazer. It was going to be my last year. Our class would be the daddies now, me and the boys.

When I went to school that first day, the beginning of the end, there were the boys. I saw Billy Kilby. I had been round to his house a few times to see the treacle that he swore came out of his taps; I had believed him. His mother was lovely. I'd been to Jimmy Burke's house out in Birstall. He came from money, Jimmy did. There was John Connor, too. I'd visited him, gone for tea. John O'Connor was a bit shy towards me. I thought, *What's up with ye, John?* John could draw great pictures of pirate ships, galleons. I'd take them home, show everyone, and swear I'd done them.

His reticence took a little while for me to fathom, but then I found out that I'd given him nits. His mother told him not to go anywhere near me. Being the sort of honest, decent guy John was, he would nod and talk, but there was no comradeship. I missed John. There was still Billy Kilby, though. I had another scrap with him and broke my glasses. The opticians warned me that if I had to take my glasses in one more time, we'd have to start paying for them. It was getting ridiculous. The shop was in Charles Street and I'd have to take the morning off school to go in and get them mended, and pick up a temporary pair. I was also wearing a patch over one eye by this time, to correct a 'lazy' eye.

Morrissey, Jerry, Chris Griffin, Bairdy, Pat Greesley, Steve Sherrard and me – we were the boys, enjoying the girls all giggling at us, fancying this one or that one. They were all into Cliff Richard. Pete Kavanaugh was back. He looked like he'd never been out of his school uniform, like he'd slept in it for the past two months. He stank like a pig, but was quiet as a mouse, always sucking his fingers.

John's first day at English Martyrs was not a success. He didn't like it. Obviously, there had been the usual first years' scare stories about getting heads pushed down the toilet by the big kids, all that malarkey. Luckily, he had enough friends that left St Pat's with him to help him cope with this new world. Pete Davis was his best mate. This was also John's Confirmation year, when you get to choose an extra name to sign up as an adult honourable Christian soldier. John picked Peter, after St Peter and his fine friend.

That last year for me at St Pat's felt a bit odd. We sort of drifted through. We had all left for our summer holidays and when we got back for that final year, we all seemed pretty grown up. Those games of cowboys and Indians we used to play seemed far too silly. We knew we were going to be separated, some to English Martyrs, some over to Corpus Christi. Belgrave Road was the dividing line that decided where you went. If you lived on the left side, it was English Martyrs, if you lived across the road, it was Corpus Christi. My old mate, Peter Michael, 'Birdie', John O'Connor, Gerald O' Boyd, Pete Cavanaugh, and the Morrisseys were all Corpus Christi.

We had to take the Eleven Plus exams, to see if we could go to the grammar school. I failed – no surprise there. Then it seemed, before we blinked, that we were on the bus for the last time, sadly saying goodbye to all our friends.

The six-or-seven-week holiday loomed. What was I to do? It started off normally; I had a paper round by then. Arthur Boyle fixed me up with that. He was the eldest of the five Boyle brothers and the one girl: Arthur, Roger, Tony, Billy, Geoff and Elaine. A lovely family. The mum worked in a factory. You didn't mess with her. She usually had a cigarette hanging out of her mouth. Their dad worked down in the wholesale market. We'd often go down on a Saturday morning to see him. He'd give us a bunch of bananas. They weren't ripe, but we didn't mind. We'd still eat them.

The holidays went by pretty quickly. Arthur and I would be up every morning at 5.30 to catch the 6.05 bus to go and collect our sack of papers. He had a good round, the shortest, which is fair enough since he got me the job. I managed to keep that job for the next two years. It was hard work, on Wednesdays especially. That was magazine day. The sack was so heavy the strap would cut into your shoulder. I had to drag it along, and when it was icy, God, it was hard. We were on about 17/6 a week, that's about 80p, and he'd give us five fags on a Monday. On spring days it was good to be up before everybody else, but in winter it was pitch dark and horrible. I envied the rest of the family, all snug and warm, tucked in their beds.

Chapter Sixteen

English Martyrs

That last summer between St Pat's and going up to English Martyrs seemed to fly by. We had drifted through our days going fishing or horsing around in the fields. When we were in that last year, we'd felt all grown up. At the end of those eight weeks I was kitted out in my first long trousers, part of my free English Martyrs uniform. It was a rite of passage, but on arriving at the school, we immediately knew we were now at the bottom of the heap, the little ones. Luckily, most of us had an older brother or sister already there to show us the ropes and look out for us. Although this school had over six hundred pupils from all over, I always felt safe there.

When I started, the school had only been built about eighteen months. I watched two coaches pull up and unload kids from Market Harborough. The school was required to take in ten per cent non-Catholics, but there were no Asian students. It was mostly Irish, Polish and Italians. Some of the Italian girls were quite dark, but I only ever knew one black student, Peter Dorfleur, who had been adopted by Irish parents and was, without doubt, as black as coal. He was a year older than me, in John's year. I managed to get into a fight with him for the understandable reason that I called him a 'black bastard', which in hindsight was unwise as well as plain stupid and wrong. But at that age I spoke first and thought about it later, if at all. John managed to have a word with Peter and told him to let it go.

I suppose my mates and I were 'angels with dirty faces', not bad lads, just a little rough around the edges. I was a regular smoker by then and a gang of us, all ages, hung out behind the gym at break times. Of course, if you were caught smoking, you were caned. That wasn't the only physical punishment. Our PE teacher, Mr Smith, preferred a size 10 plimsoll (slipper) whacked across our bottom, mostly earned by talking back, being cheeky, getting into fights, or for bullying. There wasn't much bullying. If you were caught fighting, both of you got the slipper.

Kids will always have cliques or gangs. By Christmas I reckon I was Number Two in the pecking order. There was only one guy in our year who had more clout. The newness had worn off; we had all learned how to play the game and fit into the system. The school was strict.

I was placed in the middle stream academically. I did alright. My House Master was Mr Goodall, a science teacher, who would also later teach my son and daughter. He was quite tough, but he needed to be to sort us lot out. Courses change with the times. I was taught English, History (which never mentioned Irish history even though the Troubles were spilling into our lives), Geography, RE, Science, Maths, PE twice a week, Music once a week, plus Woodwork, Metalwork and Technical Drawing. The girls, of course, were sent off to Domestic Science. I was never into sport, although having the right boots might have helped – any boots – but the playing fields at English Martyrs were glorious wide-open spaces, after the two cramped paved areas with a bit of apparatus we made do with at St Pat's.

My school day started at 8.45 for Registration. Then we all piled into assembly for nine o'clock. The headmaster was 'Bulldog' Mulvey, who looked just like a bulldog to us. Mr Connolly was the deputy head. He was tall with jet black hair, handsome. In his spare time he was very active supporting ex-prisoners in the Halfway House on Dover Street. Mr Eliot taught RE, as did Mrs Kennedy. We used to distract Mr Eliot by getting him to talk about the injustices in Northern Ireland. He was very nice. Mrs Woods taught History. She didn't think much of me. I ran into her again years later when Pam and I were on holiday, and she made sure to let me know how she felt.

There were two Mr Haneys, cousins. One taught English and was very tough on our John. It has to be said, John was a typical scruff at this time. One of his more dapper mates used to hand on decent clothes to him, but when John wore them, it was all a mess. He was too gangly and restless, never at ease. He wanted so badly to be a rebel, a Hell's Angel. Nothing could make him look tidy, and that suited him just fine. It seems incredible and would not be allowed in today's classrooms, but that Mr Haney lost patience with John's refusal to cut his hair, so he forcibly cut his hair in front of the whole class. Not exactly a tactic to encourage John to consider pursuing his education. The other Mr Haney was a small fellow with glasses who taught Music. I never had much time for Music, had no singing voice, and wasn't interested in playing an instrument either. The teacher used to tell me to just sit the lesson out. John, however, was mad on music. He was nuts about the Beatles and the Stones. This was their heyday, around the mid to late sixties. Poor John even tried to make himself a guitar out of wood from an orange crate and some piano wire. He could mimic Mick Jagger and even performed his Jagger routine years later at our wedding.

Back then, there were separate areas for girls and boys at break, with teachers patrolling us. Dinner was held in a couple of shifts. At the end of the afternoon, the final bell would ring at 3.45 and I'd be off on the bus. I had to pay, but at least my uniform was free and I still had free school dinners. If asked what I liked best about school, I'd have to admit it was the dinners. Some of my mates stayed on after school for football and other activities, but I went straight for the bus and usually managed to get my homework done on the journey. Schoolwork didn't interest me; I just got it out of the way.

When I got home our tea would be on the table and Mam would be out, off down the bookie's or the bingo. If there was no telly, she'd be bored. She needed something in her life. I used to scrounge down the back of the settee to find odd change. Mam never bought a new settee – we always had ones the neighbours were getting shot of. We had a slew of them out back. Mam could never refuse a donated one, but never bothered to get rid of the others. We'd attack every new donation because there was bound to be money down the back. If we were bored, we could have our own little bonfire with the odd redundant settee.

By the time I was in secondary school, summer holidays spent larking about making swings in the trees seemed pretty tame. The 'in' thing was to have a catapult. There was a gang of about twenty of us. I was one of the younger ones in this group, mostly all Irish lads looking for something to do. We decided to break a few windows with our catapults and headed off to Mowmacre School, which was on the estate quite close by. We attacked the Juniors and Infants and just about smashed every window in the place.

On Sundays we used to walk to Braggie (Bradgate Park), which wasn't that far away. We'd pack ourselves some jam sandwiches and bring along bottles of water. As we came through Anstey, we'd loot the sweet shop, stuffing our pockets with as many sweets as we could before we were chased off. I remember one time in Anstey, Brian Oliver, Mark Rioco, Mick Clements and I decided to break into the telephone exchange, a big old building, just to see what was inside, see if there was anything we fancied. We heard noises, machines. We snaffled a few trophy items, but we weren't sure what the gadgets were.

In another escapade we broke into Beaumont Leys School, looking for cigarettes or money. We caused mayhem, running round every classroom. One of my mates knew a kid from this school and hated him, so he decided to send him a message by shitting in his desk.

We even broke into the headmaster's office and tried on his cap and gown. We only managed to find about one pound and ten cigarettes, but I reckon we did those pupils a service, because before we left we smashed his entire collection of canes.

Our mini crime wave did not go unnoticed and came to an abrupt end. Wild as we were, our exploits were no worse than most estates at the time. A big Scottish cop, John McCorkendale, was sent to put a stop to it all. Mam loved him; he was a strong fellow, man enough to tackle the rowdiness and sort us out. It didn't take long, what with a bit of helpful grassing. We all got done for the whole lot, and were sent to Juvenile Court, which was then on Vestry Street.

When I appeared in court, I actually fainted. I thought I was going to be sent to Approved School. But two of our gang ran away and when they were eventually caught, they were actually sent to Approved School. I was only about twelve at the time, and most of us were put on probation for two years. We had to meet our probation officer all together in the Community Centre every second Tuesday, when he'd listen to how we were getting on.

Needless to say, Mr Mulvey went up the wall. He was livid. We were forced to face big Gus, who was the very frightening caretaker at Mowmacre School, which had been our first bit of vandalism. We were beginning to feel ashamed. It was to Mulvey's credit that he never sent us to Beaumont Leys to apologise. I dread to think what that would have been like.

I remember that Mick Clements and I went to see *Mary Poppins* the Sunday when he returned from Approved School. He had been one of the lads that ran away. The film had just come out. An innocent choice for rowdy lads, perhaps, but we loved going to the cinema every Sunday and watched whatever was on.

Chapter Seventeen

Getting On

Since the three of us, John, me, and Mary are each only eleven months apart, it meant that Mary started at English Martyrs as I entered Year 8. She was subdued and seemed to go along with the system in that first year. It's important to understand that everyone felt interconnected. There were O'Briens, Carrolls … everyone seemed to be someone or other's cousin. Our parents were all connected, interrelated. It was a small, close world.

Mary behaved herself at first. As time went on, her attitude changed. She became cheekier and started truanting. She never finished school. Mary wouldn't give in and play along with the system as she grew older. When I left, there was no one to keep an eye on her. In the end, they threw her out.

At fourteen, I went down to Wembley with Chris Griffin and Keith Harrison. They were part of our gang, along with Matt Corham, 'Boney' Carroll, Mick O'Hara, Spike, and Carl Anderson, who happened to be Englebert Humperdinck's nephew. Since this was Englebert's heyday, that was a big deal. Keith, by the way, had asked me round to his house one day after school. He noticed I was out of funds to buy any more cigarettes. 'I've got some round mine,' he said.

It was only a stone's throw from the school, so over I went. 'How many you got?'

'About eighteen thousand,' he mumbled rather quietly. Stolen from a railway, apparently, and kept tucked away by his mum, aiding and abetting her dodgy boyfriend.

The aftermath of my probation affected my remaining time at school, but in rather bizarre ways. We had a young teacher for Drama one year, a Miss Burrows, who fancied herself as a bit of a hippy type. She was easy to get off track and we encouraged her to ramble on about various exotic substances she might have inhaled. During one lesson I came in for special praise. She set us a role-play exercise: bank robberies. I excelled myself! Apparently my interpretation was realistic and convincing, and my use of chairs and desks to suggest scene changes was quite brilliant!

The O'Sullivans definitely had a flair for performing. John entertained whole classrooms with his storytelling even in primary school. He was known as a great entertainer all his life. The nasty Mr Haney used that skill quite ruthlessly after my trial. He set up a mock trial in his classroom and had John re-enact the whole thing. When it was my turn to have him for English, I was tormented too.

As our period of probation came to an end, the gang all went in different directions. We'd evolved to like different music, different styles, and some had opted to start smoking dope. I was smoking and drinking, and in nightclubs at fourteen. No one seemed bothered about checking my age. I was hanging out with older kids. I didn't like the taste of beer, but it was where the action was, and where I wanted to be.

For all my pretend adulthood, I wasn't really that bothered with girls yet. Oh, the girls noticed me alright; I had a following. I can modestly admit that two girls actually fought over me. I was sought after, but I was too shy, although that changed a year or so later.

When John left school, he was apprenticed to an upmarket painter and decorator. Everyone left with a job to go to. It may not have been the job people stayed in, but we had a start. Ninety per cent of the Irish went into the building trades. They had fathers, uncles, cousins, older brothers already there to offer them a place. John only lasted a week. They insisted he smarten up his appearance and get his hair cut. John refused.

The girls were all sent into the hosiery firms. There was never any thought of a career – only a handful went on to further education. The best had already been creamed off and sent to grammar school.

'Bulldog' Mulvey left. His replacement as headmaster was my old head at St Pat's, Mr Brennan, the man who said he'd pay for me to get my hair cut. He was an interesting man. I think he must have seen something in me, something worth bothering about. He didn't just write me off as a troublemaker. Towards the end of my time at English Martyrs, he decided that Chris Griffin and I should help with the morning assemblies. He initially described it as a sort of punishment, but I liked the trust he placed in us. I used to try and beat him to the front, and start the prayers before he was there. I ended up with a decent relationship with Mr Brennan.

My old RE teacher, Mrs Kennedy, must be nearly ninety now, but I see her now and again. She's still in touch with Mr Brennan, and I hope he knows I've turned out just fine, with a grand, loving family, and have made something of myself. I totally enjoyed my fourth year. When I left English Martyrs I was still only fourteen, almost fifteen. I loved my time there and was genuinely sad to leave.

That says something about the quality of the place, and the people who cared for us.

PART TWO

Chapter Eighteen

Getting Ahead of Myself

That last few weeks of school, no one cared much about anything but getting free, getting out into the adult world of work. We wasted away days clearing up desks, setting the place straight after our mess. Some even took to burning their school blazers as a crude rite of passage. We were 'gate happy', prisoners of the system aching to be let loose on the jobs laid on for us. Only a couple of lads, Peter Blackall, whose dad was a principal officer at Welford Road prison, and Michael Keenan, a lad from rural Ireland, were kept back. Pete was bright enough, but probably had something like dyslexia, which wasn't picked up on then. They had to complete one more year to hit the leaving standard.

    I had managed to play the grown-up game long before the July break-up. I'd got myself a job as a kitchen porter at the Bell Hotel. They didn't seem too bothered about checking my age. If I could handle the work and was reliable, no bother. That whole last year at school I was quietly moving up the ranks at the Bell. I started by just feeding the dishwashing machines, keeping the mountain of dirty dinnerware moving through. I was a good worker and ended up sorting the rotas for the whole crew.

Hotel kitchens took on a pretty fluid staff. No one stayed long; people drifted in and out. It was a sweaty, messy job. In a time before mobile phones, before most of the guys in that kitchen would have had a permanent address or landline, if someone didn't show up, we had to find someone else, almost anyone else, damn quick. I could do that. A mate of mine got me the job, and I, in turn, could get work for friends. I have always been quick to learn how to be useful, and how a system works. Exams don't teach you that. It's a survival strategy.

I did better than survive. I made good money. It was only ten pence an hour, but the hours added up. On Christmas Day it was time and a half and busy all day. They even sent a taxi to fetch me. The food, of course, was fantastic. We ate what the guests ate, even for banquets, just a few hours earlier.

Sunday afternoons were usually quiet, and most staff were off. We hung around in the staff quarters in the cellar for those few hours, waiting for the evening shift to start. No one seemed to remember to cut off the beer taps up in the bar when they went home, so we stragglers had a blissful few beers with our feet up, hoping no one would catch on. Someone eventually grassed, but we were only given a slapped wrist over the business. They valued dependable crew and didn't want to sack us. I carried on at the Bell until June 1969. It was then pulled down to build the new Haymarket shopping centre. The Bell used to stand opposite the old Lewis's.

This little sideline had me hanging out with men who were on average nine to eleven years older than me. This became the group I spent more and more time with. They got me into supporting football – Leicester City, of course. I was a skinhead. Peter Blackham, the friend of mine from school, got me a ticket to the Leicester Cup

Final at Wembley that May, playing Manchester City. It only cost me 12/6 (about 65p).

So when the apprenticeship to Universal Plasterers turned up for me, I wasn't jumping for joy. I gave it a try, but it was still at the going rate of ten pence per hour with, as far as I could see, very few perks. John had lost his job as a decorator because he wouldn't cut his hair, and was at this time working in a shoe factory as a labourer. Since we were both at work, Mam demanded we paid for our board. She was hoping for £5 from each of us, but as we only earned £4 a week, she had to settle for only £3. Only one pound a week for my personal use was not much to fund a social life.

Mam packed up my cheese and spam sandwiches and off I set to report to Mr Buncer at UP's Wharf Street office. This was a well-established firm, with about ten on the payroll.

I quickly deduced that all they wanted me to do was to mix the plaster, ready for the skilled men to do the actual plastering. I received no training, hadn't a clue how to even hold a trowel. We'd get sent out to churches and places out in the middle of nowhere to plaster, and I'd be huddled in the back of a van, scrunched up and bumped alongside all the gear, having to set up and get mixing long before the others had to start.

As the new boy, I was sent on all manner of fool's errands for a 'glass hammer', a 'long weight' or off to a nearby butcher's for 'blackcurrant dripping'. But it was hard work. Apprenticeships also required four years' study, spent in two-week blocks at full-time technical colleges. As full-time courses, they also included PE lessons. When I started my first session that September, the course trainers soon realised I had been taught no basic skills by my employer. This was around the time when the skinhead trend came in. It started in London and we copied it. At the start it was hobnailed boots, jeans, braces and a denim jacket – that was the uniform.

The cold weather was setting in. The thought of a lifetime of this sort of graft did not appeal to me one iota. Some apprenticeships did succeed. Chris Griffin went into chef training. Years later he invited us down to join him in Australia for the millennium. Several of my mates stayed with the building trades and have done well for themselves. It just wasn't for me.

My job started at half seven in the morning and we were off by four, so one afternoon I slipped into the youth employment office and asked for a change. I was offered a chance to work for a self-employed carpet fitter. He came to our house to interview me in front of Mam. She wasn't keen, worried I'd measure up wrong. Fussing, she was. I was interested. I'd be working in interesting places, in the warm. I took to it. There was a downside, however: he worked all hours. There were hardly any weekends off – unless Leicester City were playing at home. Thank God he was a Leicester fan!

Chapter Nineteen

My Skinhead Days

I was a Leicester City supporter. We always used to get the bus in Humberstone Gate facing the Three Cranes, which we made our headquarters. All the lads would be in there, a few old faces from St Pats. We would get the bus to the away games, and then afterwards meet up in the Three Cranes and reminisce. It was great fun at the time.

Our gang would meet up with the boys from the Cranes; they had a good table football team – that was the sport at the time. We would go in, get a drink and play table football.

I would see some old school pals. The Brennans were there; the older one, Tony, had his own gang. Pat Bunce, Steve Marvel, Brian Durkin, and John Regan were ex-Corpus-Christi lads.

John Regan was obsessed with the City. A few years later he got married on a Monday so he didn't miss a game. We were friends for years, and fifty years later he ended up working for me at my bar as a barman. Those were the days.

Away days were the best. We would all meet there, excited. We were still in the first division. The previous year we'd gone to Wembley, lost to Manchester City, but now it was a case of survival.

We'd got about three games left, and one was Sheffield United away. The coach broke down on the way back on the M1. In those days when a coach broke down it broke down, and that was that!

Tom Amoroso got off the coach. He took off his coat and made out he was a matador, bull fighting the cars. The police came, Yorkshire police, a big sergeant laying down the law. He arrested John Regan, dragging him off the coach. I think a couple more of the lads got arrested too. But in those days they seemed to do it just to get on your nerves.

We eventually got back. John Regan had to appear in court. It was nothing serious – abusive language or something like that.

The last game of the season was at Manchester United, and if we lost we would be relegated. We went to Old Trafford on the coaches and we lost the game.

After the game we were chatting with some of the home fans. They said, 'You better get off now, lads, here come the Scarf Hawks.' We looked round towards the home stand and it seemed like the whole of the Stretford End was walking round the ground towards us.

In those days you could go into the ground at one end and walk all the way round. It wasn't really fenced off, and they did look a motley mob. Anyway, we managed to get back to the coach, and the next season we were in division two.

We were in town, in the Three Cranes with all the lads, when – and I will never forget this – Ernie walked through the door. He was a big, tall lad, known as Ernie Bollockhead. He was great mates with Pat Bunce, John Regan and the boys. He was also ex-Corpus

Christi, and he had actually had a full skinhead, a shaven head. He was so funny. Anyway, he set the trend.

We left the pub that day to go on a pub crawl. A car load of coppers pulled up, didn't ask any questions, just grabbed hold of Ernie, threw him in the back of the car and drove off.

It turned out they had spotted him and they presumed, because of his haircut, that he had escaped from borstal. That was the sort of impression that haircut gave. Anyway, once he had explained they let him go. After that we all decided to have the real skinhead.

I remember going home and Mam took one look at me and smacked me round the head. 'Jesus Christ, Timmy, what have you done with your curls, your beautiful black curls?'

'This is the fashion, Mam.'

'Fashion? I'll give you fashion.'

Anyway, I got whole 'Holy Mary mother of God. God Almighty, what has he done to himself?'

But it soon grew back – my hair did grow fast – and after that I just kept it tidy, still skinheadish, but a lot of the lads still went for the full bore.

On the fashion scene, the jeans stayed but the hobnailed boots had to go. The cockney lads were wearing Doc Martens, beautiful boots, all shined up perfect. Soldiers wore them, policemen did; they lasted forever, but they were expensive. But you weren't anybody unless you wore your Doc Martens, Sta-Prest trousers, dog-tooth preferably, braces, Ben Sherman shirts. Now they were expensive – the first one I bought cost me £3.

When I told Mam how much it had cost she screamed her head off. 'God Almighty, do you realise what I have to do for £3?'

'Mam,' I said, 'the days of me accepting rags from the neighbours have gone. I'll save up and buy my own clothes.'

I loved that Ben Sherman shirt. I'd have it on my back all weekend. Wear it, take it off, get it washed and put it back on again. So, that was the fashion.

One of the carpet-fitting jobs I was sent on was to an insurance office. One of the office staff caught my eye, and Helen and I started seeing each other. She didn't seem to mind the skinhead look and the fact I hung out with other skinheads at City matches. She knew I liked getting into fights, and that I hoped there'd be some excitement after matches to get stuck into. Looking back, I freely admit I had a quick temper. I was a hard worker, but not too bothered where all this grind was taking me. I was a confident enough fellow, but never set my targets very high. My attitude then was 'Let's see what comes, I'm young, and I've got my health.'

Our gang decided we wanted to change pub. The Cranes was alright, but it used to get packed with a lot of strangers and there was starting to be trouble.

I'm not sure if it was Tony Bakewell who suggested it, but we came across the Berni Steak Bar in Belgrave Gate, and downstairs was a bar, so we made that our headquarters.

We'd all be in there with the girls, Helen and her best mate Jackie, Pat Booton, a German girl, our girlfriends, and that was our HQ.

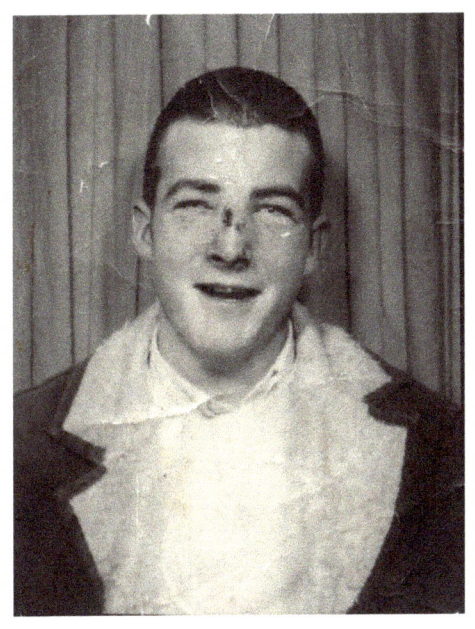

Tim in his skinhead days

The Three Cranes

A visit to London, mid 70s.
Left to right: Pete Birdie Jack Cockroft, Tim and Nick Loxley.
The car did not belong to any of them.

Chapter Twenty

Margate

Neither Helen nor I were planning ahead; we were enjoying the present, making the most of what we had. Leicester shut down for the first two weeks of July every year – the July Fortnight. Everyone went away, everyone except Mam and us. Since our family had never been able to afford this treat, I was determined to escape at last on a planned holiday. Nick Loxley, who I'd known since we met doing paper rounds, and I booked hotel rooms, and our girlfriends respectfully booked into separate accommodation. Altogether there were about fifteen or twenty of us from Leicester descending on Margate for that fortnight. I was going to celebrate my sixteenth birthday there. It was going to be magic.

Nick and I travelled down on the bus. A couple of the lads who joined us had absconded from Approved School and fancied a break in Margate. Tony and Gary Bakewell had been sentenced to attend Approved School for three years. People who absconded were re-arrested and sent back to court, but they would only be sent to a Detention Centre for either a three- or six-month stretch. It seemed a bizarre incentive for them to abscond and thereby reduce their sentence, with the added bonus of a little time off in Margate thrown in.

Everything seemed to go well. I had no trouble being served in pubs, young as I was. We got on well with the local skinheads. Helen and I were having a fine old time. The authorities, however, had noticed the Bakewells were missing and decided to raid our lively Leicester group. They picked up the brothers and then searched all our rooms for any incriminating evidence. In my room they found a bottle of Brut that I'd paid a guy in the pub £5 for. It was part of a stolen load, so I was charged with receiving stolen property. My court appearance was not scheduled until September. After Margate, it was back to work as usual, and by August the football season had returned to liven up our lives.

They were now putting on trains, Football Specials. You got on at London Road Station and off at wherever we were playing. There were police on the trains, but they got to know who you were, and there was never any major trouble.

The cockneys were smashing trains up, and the violence was getting out of hand. What they were doing on the Monday, we would be doing on the Wednesday and Thursday; it would drift up.

But the skinhead days were fading and my hair got longer.

My boss was not amused by my having to lose work to show up for a court appearance. I lost my job over that.

Work was not hard to come by if you weren't too fussy. I found a place in a plastics factory near the Belgrave flyover. I packed sheeted plastic for £6-£7 a week, working only nine to five, so the hours were better and it was decent money. I only stayed a couple of months though.

As 1969 headed towards its close, two things changed. The Bakewell boys had completed their time and were out after detention. I was having a rare old time each weekend getting stuck into any fight, smashing up pubs. Everyone was getting into trouble. That year I shamed Mam by going up to Communion at Christmas with two unmistakable black eyes.

The second notable change was that by Christmas, there was no more room for doubt. Helen was pregnant. Our child had been conceived in Margate and was due in April.

I was going to be a father at sixteen.

Margate Beach 8th July, Tim's sixteenth birthday. From left to right: standing Gary Bakewell, Kim Henson, Tim and Tony Bakewell

Chapter Twenty-One

Further Education

Not all learning comes from books. The next two years of my life were one hell of an education. I made some almighty mistakes, no doubt about it. There is nothing to admire about some of the choices I made. I thought I was clever. I thought I could duck and dive, play rough like the big boys, and get away with it. Those two years proved a mighty steep learning curve.

In the normal way of things, Helen knew long before Christmas that she was pregnant. I suppose around October she and I started talking about what we were going to do. Helen was almost twenty-one, five years older than me. She was ready to nest-build and had me in her sights for a long-term future.

She wanted the baby, and she wanted me. I had to meet her folks, Eddie and Laura. I'd never set eyes on them before. They came to terms with our predicament, and we became engaged. Mam was keen on Helen, they got on well together. She was delighted to be having a grandchild. She was very happy and was looking forward to our marriage. Eddie, my prospective father-in-law, had been a child in a German concentration camp and was a very quiet, decent man. He managed to get me a night shift refitting bookmakers' shops so that I could save up to buy Helen a ring and put some by in the Post Office for the baby. This work was on top of my day job, so I was working flat out.

We planned to marry after the baby was born, so Helen felt assured and able to flaunt her baby bulge as soon as she had her ring. By Christmas she was five months along and already huge.

I was Mam's golden boy, earning decent money, engaged to a lovely Catholic girl and about to make her a grandmother. All that was true enough, but I still wanted my freedom while I could. I liked a bit of life on the wild side, hanging out with older guys who had dodgy pasts, who'd done time. Everyone I knew was robbing, was up to something not exactly legal, on some kind of fiddle. That was my social world and I loved it.

It seemed a natural progression from those childhood days shoplifting with Norah, or with my gang of mates rushing the sweet shop to steel sweets in Anstey. Two of my mates, Graham Kemp and 'Dusty', a big lummox who played the clown, were a good four or five years older than me. They had it in mind to do over a sweet shop in town. I wasn't to do much except be last in and lock the door. Dusty would wield a hammer and Graham would threaten the owner with an imitation gun. We'd be in and out in minutes.

For a craic, I agreed. We decided to meet up the following Saturday at the George Pub by the Clock Tower for a drink before it all kicked off. Leicester City was playing at home on 13 February, and we were hoping to be mistaken for troublesome away fans. As we sat sipping our pints, I couldn't ignore how psyched up those guys were. They worried me. Then Graham suggested a slight change of plan.

'It's not going to be a sweet shop, Tim. I've had a better idea,' said Graham, winking at Dusty. 'We're going for Richardson's, the jewellers on the high street.'

'Are you fucking mad?' I asked. 'You've not cased the place, checked out the owner, or anything. It's broad daylight, in the middle of the high street and the city is bursting on a Saturday.' They laughed off my objections. Nothing was going to put them off.

I walked past the shop window before they burst in and caught sight of the owner. He was a big burly fella who looked like he could take care of himself. This was not a good idea, but before I could try and talk them out of it, they stormed in. I played my part and locked the door behind them.

Dusty waved his hammer; Graham brandished his gun. The guy read us like a book and reckoned he could take us on. I could see it in his eyes. It only took a second for him to reach under his counter for a hefty cosh. Dusty froze. I shouted to him to whack the guy, but he did nothing. The guy came at us and all hell broke loose, making a right mess of the place. Dusty and Graham tried to escape and struggled because the door had been nicely locked and bolted by yours truly. Which left me to tackle the owner. I smashed his head with one of the clocks on display. With the door finally opened, the three of us ran away empty-handed, but as I was the last one out, the owner caught the back of my head with his cosh. It opened a gash and blood poured down, soaking me.

I could feel the wetness of it running down my neck. I took off my tank top and wound it round my head to stem the flow and hide the injury. The other two had split and run off. I made a dash for Ozzie's Snooker Hall nearby. When I showed up the crowd in there could see I'd been in a spot of bother, understood my predicament, and asked no questions. They cleaned up the gash with a cold flannel and helped tidy me up. I could pass it off as trouble with those useful away fans.

I made my way home to find my two cronies waiting for me. Mam was away in Ireland at the O'Conners. I soaked my blood-stained clothes and changed into clean ones. We reckoned we got away with it, so I sauntered into town for my usual Saturday night out. On Monday the *Mercury* had a big front-page spread about the brave shop owner who foiled an attempted armed robbery. The descriptions of us were wildly inaccurate. They were on the lookout for three grown men with donkey jackets. They had no evidence – it was years before any DNA or fancy forensics. We were free and clear.

I had made up my mind that I would never fool around with these prize idiots ever again. *I'm not in for this,* I told myself. *I'm the only one of us who's actually holding down a job – two, as it happens. Taking these risks is just not worth it. If I want to get rich, the only way is to work for it.* The whole fiasco really woke me up. I had everything going for me, so why chance it all? For what? For loyalty? Loyalty to losers? What had I been thinking? Had I been thinking? Probably not, at that age. Nothing scared me then.

There was a sense that whatever happened down in London was a big deal. We tried to copy their hellraising. Every football ground had its own crop of loyal, rowdy fans. Every gang of away fans tried to take over the kop. Every other Saturday was an Away Day Out to let loose and have a go. The sort of mates you ran with in that scenario were not really focused on their long-term future. All my friends had been sent to borstal at one time or another. It was a sort of natural, expected progression. We were the rubbish on the estate. It didn't matter what happened to us. There were no positive, alternative role models.

I was about to be a father and even at sixteen I was determined that this kid of mine would not grow up starving like we had. There had to be a better way. Mam had never been any good at managing what little money came her way. I blamed her orphanage upbringing. She wasn't as institutionalised as her sister, but she was damaged, nonetheless. I watched as time and again she spent every last penny, and never seemed happy unless she was skint. John was supposed to give her £3 a week from his wages, but he hid money from her and always came up with a charming excuse as to why he couldn't pay his share. Mary was running riot, up to all sorts. If things were going to change, it was down to me.

Chapter Twenty-Two

Spring 1970

Two weeks later there was a knock at the door. Mam answered and I was shouted down. 'It's CID for you, Tim.' John McCorkindale, the policeman who'd rounded up our gang and knew us all very well, the strong authoritative fella my mother always fancied, had come for a chat.

It started all friendly. 'I hear you're doing well, Tim, with a good job.' He knew I was about to be a dad too. Then the conversation gently turned to where I was that Saturday afternoon.

'In town, as usual,' I replied.

'Nowhere near Richardson's the jewellers on the high street, by any chance?' He was giving me a chance to own up. I didn't take it.

Mam stopped smiling. When he realised I wasn't cooperating, he asked to look at my head.

'Why?' asked Mam.

'Because I expect I'll find a three-inch gash inflicted by the shop owner on the last of the three armed robbers as he escaped after attempting to rob his shop.'

He found the raw scar easily enough. The game was up.

Mam then compounded my guilt by piping up, 'I wondered what all those blood-soaked clothes were doing under the sink.'

I'd forgotten all about them, and never rinsed them out. Mam was in shock.

McCorkindale told me that dear old Graham Kemp was up on remand in Welford prison. He was terrified of a gate arrest, being arrested the minute he was released for serving time for his current offence, for other misdeeds that had just caught up with him. He coughed up everything he'd ever done, just to be sure.

Mam came with me to Charles Street police station where I was charged and bailed. I pleaded guilty and was remanded to the Assizes Court, which was due to sit in May. I was no longer her golden boy. Her John, who could charm the birds out of the trees and free drinks out of every pub, John the great storyteller, became the only one who could bring a smile to light her life.

Out on bail, I carried on with my life as usual, going out with friends to the pub at weekends, getting into the odd scrap, chatting up girls. I wasn't married yet. I didn't see the harm in it; as long as they knew about Helen and the baby, knew that no relationship was possible. On 10 April, Easter Sunday, I had just returned from Mass with Mam, still in my white shirt and sporting my weekend's black eye, when Eddie and Laura rang the doorbell.

'Helen's had a little boy.' He was a fine seven pounder, born over in Kirby Muxloe hospital. Helen was kept in a week, which was the norm then. I managed to get over once to see them. I had less than a month to get to know my son before I was due in court.

Everyone was optimistic about my chances. I was only sixteen with a new baby. Unlike my co-defendants, I did not have a string of offences chalked up against me. Surely, the judge would be lenient.

Spring 1970

I went down to the Castle courtrooms on the bus. Mam was working and was joining me later; Helen made her own way there. I remember thinking, *Is this the last time I walk through these streets?* The place was full to bursting with officials in full regalia. It was a very solemn and impressive occasion. Only the most serious crimes were referred to this court, which only sat every six months. Some of my friends showed up. Kemp was kept down in the cells, but Dusty had been out on bail like me. We hadn't spoken since the incident. Twenty-seven people were up before the judge that day, quite a few for armed robbery – a gang of fearsome black guys from Northampton and another gang from Hinckley among them. Helen and I had been chatting about taking the baby out to the park for a stroll in the afternoon, we were feeling that confident. That confidence took a knock when I saw the tough customers I was being lined up with.

Two big limousines pulled up and the police inspectors stood to attention. Heralds in full rig-out sounded a fanfare. A small civil servant carrying a sceptre preceded the judge who was in his full robes and wig. This august procession was halted when the old judge tripped on his gown, and all the criminals who stood by watching the ceremony burst out laughing. A spontaneous reaction, but perhaps not wise. As this was a court session to determine sentencing, jeering at the judge was not recommended as a route to leniency.

I was called in at 11 a.m. I had watched others go in before me, and no one came out. They all went down to the cells. It was a very old dock, grand and impressive.

We had all pleaded guilty and were given three years each. Mrs Horner, my wonderful probation officer, reminded the judge that I was only sixteen and that sentence could not apply to me. It was commuted to two years in borstal, to serve the full term. This also went against the regulations, because I should not be denied the chance to earn remission for good behaviour, and she sorted that out too.

As the sentence was read out, I admit I really wanted my mam then. I watched Kemp being taken down, smirking. He'd got the same sentence for a host of crimes, and he was the one who'd dropped me in it. I decided there and then that this was not my game. *Fuck me, this is it.*

I was taken to Welford Road first, but as soon as they started processing me, it was discovered that I was too young to be there. Arrangements were set in motion to have me taken by taxi down to Wormwood Scrubs. It took two days for that to be organised, and in the meantime some of my older mates at Welford Road managed to get little welcome presents of tobacco and soap sent to cheer me up. I appreciated that.

Usually, the holding time in the Scrubs was about two weeks, while a place nearer home was found. It took much longer before I was assigned to Wellingborough, which was a closed prison built on the H-block design. I enjoyed the work and was signed up for literacy classes too. The teachers found I was too bright for their sessions: some of those young men couldn't even write their own names.

I had lost my carpet-fitting job because of my (then) forthcoming court appearance, but I had intended to leave anyway because my boss worked all hours and I had no life, no spare time. A fridge company had taken me on to help make deliveries. They paid well enough and worked regular hours. I never seemed to have a problem finding work or being valued by my employers. Would that still be true when I came out?

Chapter Twenty-Three

Wormwood Scrubs

As the taxi pulled into Du Cane Road, where Wormwood Scrubs sits in the west end of London, it was a formidable sight, set back off from the road, and it looked grim. It had taken hours to get there, the delay caused not so much by the distance, but by the London traffic.

When they got to the gate, the driver sounded the horn once. One gate opened. The taxi drove in and the two screws got us out, me and this other lad, uncuffed us, handed us over to the Wormwood Scrubs guards and left. We were then ordered into reception.

Wormwood Scrubs is an old Victorian building. It was grim and it was meant to be. It scared the life out of me at sixteen years of age.

It had four wings, A, B, C and D; the borstal wing was B-Wing. It contained five to six hundred lads. D-Wing was for lifers. It was a big prison. At reception we were ordered to strip off, no talking, see the doctor, touch your toes so the doctor could look up your arse to see if you had anything hidden.

You collected your uniform; if it didn't fit – tough!

I was taken to B-Wing reception, then put into a cell on the landing to be assessed in the morning. I remember my first night there. All I did was think of Mam; I said my prayers, begged, begged for God to get me through this.

The next morning, new arrivals were assessed more thoroughly, working out how far you'd got with your education, weeding out the poor kids that would be bullied. They tried to do what they thought was right. If you couldn't read they would teach you. If you couldn't write, they'd teach you.

When that was all done, I was told that I would be going to Wellingborough Borstal, a closed borstal in Northamptonshire. Then I was assigned a cell up on the threes, the third landing.

There were four landings and they were long, very long. You were not allowed to cross them, you had to walk all the way round. There were bridges on them, but they were for the guards. There were also nets, so that if anyone threw themselves over, the nets would catch them.

In the morning they would shout 'Out' and I had to leave my cell. In this cell I had a chair, a small table, a bed, a picture frame for pinning any posters on and a piss pot to piss and shit in.

Each morning the day started with slop-out. They would open the cells and I would stand in a line with the pot, sling it into the big sink, swill it out, then get a cup of tea. I would collect hot water in my jug and my razor blade and go back to my cell to wash, shave and get ready for breakfast.

When the cell door opened, I handed back the razor blade, then stood in line ready to be marched down for breakfast. As I was always hungry, I was ready for it! Once I had fetched breakfast, it was back to my cell. Later they opened the door of my cell, I put my tray out, they closed the door and that was it. That went on for my first two weeks. They came for us one afternoon, led us out and took us to the gym. We had to do a Black Circuit. Exercises on benches, press-ups, step-ups, sit-ups; it lasted about twenty-five minutes and it was exhausting. When they took me back to my cell every bone and muscle in my body ached. We had been doing nothing for two weeks but sitting in our cells. But I remember the Black Circuit, remember it well; I thought I would never get through it. Three sets of each exercise, ten press-ups, ten step-ups, ten sit-ups, and then you would do it again.

A couple of days later they got us to work. We'd get marched to one of the sheds in the prison. The job was splitting up the contactors for the telephone exchange. There were small pieces of platinum in them. We didn't have to get the platinum out of them, just strip them down to a certain size, so it was easier for whoever it was who got them, wherever they went to after us.

At least it got us out of our cells for a few hours.

Then we were marched back to our cells. We would get a cup of tea and a biscuit at eight o'clock.

I read a lot, and that got me by. Some of the lucky ones who knew somebody who would lend them a radio were the envy of the wing.

People were coming and going all the time. If you were waiting for an open borstal, you might only be there for five days. By now I'd been in there for over a month. I still had no date when I would be leaving. Every day people came in from all over the country. I got to know a few of the lads.

By the time I got to Wormwood Scrubs, Gary and Tony Bakewell had left, and Keith Harrison had left for Wellingborough. That was three of them. Birdie had gone to an open borstal in Nottingham. I was the last one to come through out of our gang.

One day, I was coming down for dinner after work and I spotted Paul Thorn on the landing at reception with about six or seven other Leicester fellows. Thornie was about my age, seventeen, and I shouted to him.

We had exercise every day for about an hour, walking around the yard. We all did it, apart from the lads who were working in the kitchens. We'd all meet up. Thornie was waiting to go to a borstal with his best mate Terry Green, a Northfields kid, Bunny Green's brother, and it was nice to have friendly faces to bring me up to speed.

I was due a visit by then. We were allowed one visit a month and the visiting time was twenty minutes. I think I managed to get two in at the Scrubs. Helen came the first time on her own on the train. She was bang on time. We only had twenty minutes, which wasn't long, but it was nice to see a friendly face. Visitors weren't allowed to bring anything in like gifts. But I had my first wages by then, so I had my tobacco and soap, plus I had saved some of my soap and tobacco from Welford Road. I had pretty much accepted by now that this was it.

Helen said that she was going to write to the Governor at Wellingborough and see if he would release me for Christmas, so that I could have the first Christmas with my son. I don't think she got much of a reply.

We were allowed one letter a week and we could only write to the people who wrote to us. Helen wrote every day, which was nice, but when I wrote back I didn't really have much to say – 'Got up, slopped out,' and that was that really.

Finally, they had me into the office and told me Wellingborough was ready for me, there was a place for me. I would be going in a week's time. I was over the moon. Things were a lot more relaxed at borstal. I had been seven weeks at Wormwood Scrubs and by then I was ready for the off.

Sundays were the worst. I went to Mass every Sunday. Then I would stand at the window, throwing scraps of food to the birds and thinking, *Would you want to swap places with me?* They would eat the bread and fly off.

From my cell window, I could see men wandering around, escapees with yellow stripes on their uniform, handcuffed to two guards – men knowing their sentence was going to be a hell of a lot longer than mine was going to be. You could multiply it by ten, probably.

Things started to ease up on my mental state, because I was looking forward to Wellingborough. The day came and I went into reception, got out of my stinking Wormwood Scrubs prison uniform and put my suit back on. Oh, it felt good to be back in my own suit, shirt, tie and shoes.

They loaded us onto a bus; I was handcuffed to some older bloke. The coach left London and travelled north, with drop-offs on the way. I remember the guy that I was handcuffed to had only one leg. I had read about him. They had found him on a railway line – his leg had been chopped off by the train. He told them that he was trying to save a dog. The *News of The World* picked up on it. It was news, how this guy had lost his leg. They organised a collection for him and he ended up getting thousands. He moaned all the way to Gartree maximum security prison.

Years later, he tried to repeat the same stunt. He was a conman and was jailed again.

When we eventually arrived at Wellingborough, we were driven in and met at reception. The doors opened and four of us got off the bus to see beautiful green grass. It was a spotless borstal. The screws were ever so nice, polite and nice. We were told that we had to take a bath; we were strip-searched and saw the doctor and that was it.

Chapter Twenty-Four

Borstal

On the day I arrived, one of the screws, Moran, said to me, 'O'Sullivan, Leicester. I hope you can play football like the guy whose cell you're taking.' He was referring to Noel Moran, who left the day I landed and I took his cell. And I had to inform him, 'No, Mr Moran, I am no sporting man.'

Once we'd got our borstal uniforms on they divided us up. Me and Baggie, one of the black fellows from Northampton, were sent to C-Wing.

There were four wings at Wellingborough – A, B, C and D. A-Wing was for the sort of kids that might be bullied, weak kids. B-Wing was run-of-the-mill, and was where Tony and Gary Bakewell were. C-Wing was for violent inmates and D-Wing was for the off-the-wall inmates, or that was the impression I got. Keith Harrison was in D-Wing.

They took us up to the dining room – they'd just served dinner. Everyone was sitting down eating, and me and Baggie walked in. The whole room went very quiet. We could tell they were weighing us up. I later found out that there was a lot of tension on C-Wing between the blacks and the whites, and the way they saw it they'd got one of each.

We walked up with our trays. I had gone through a lot of bollocks at Wormwood Scrubs with people stealing my food. That wasn't going to happen again, so I thought I'd start as I meant to go on. A big muscle-bound black guy was dishing out the chips, and when he put the chips on my plate I said to him, 'More chips, darky.' The next thing I knew, I was knocked completely across the dining room by a screw; he'd punched me straight in the face.

He told me to get up and said, 'There's no dinner for you, O'Sullivan.' So I sat down at a table, which was going to be my place for my time at borstal.

At the table there were three guys, Paddy Byrnes, a Catholic kid from Scotland, Frank Moore, an Irish kid from London, and a Welsh guy, Ellis I think his name was. One of them said, 'That was a good move, weren't it?'

I said, 'Well, you know.'

They said, 'Do you realise who he is? He's called Titus. He's the gym orderly and he's the daddy of the nick.'

Well, fuck me, I thought, *I couldn't have made a worse start.* But fortunately for me, Titus was being discharged in two weeks. He'd done his time, and the last thing he wanted was any aggro. The minimum you could lose at Wellingborough was two weeks. (On the garden party there was a guy who ate the peas instead of picking them, and he lost two weeks. Anything you did, the minimum was two weeks.) So when we went back to the wing and I was allocated a cell, I went over and apologised to him.

He didn't actually seem that bothered. I was out of order. I've been called a bogtrotter and a Paddy. It made me see red. Titus and I shared a world where 'No blacks, No Irish, No dogs' signs were common in lodging house windows. We were both unwanted outcasts. 'Darky' was the name the Irish always used. It wasn't like 'black bastard' or anything. Doing what the Irish have always done doesn't make it right, though.

Titus could see I was a cocky newbie trying to sound tough. It was an act. A wrong move, but he must have realised the kid had the guts to apologise. Anyway, he was alright about it and I breathed a big sigh of relief.

We were on the bottom rung of the ladder, the internees; those first two weeks at Wellingborough were the induction. We were given a blue tie to wear, and that meant you were bottom. There were blue, green and brown ties, and brown was discharge. But for two weeks we were bottom of the pack. We were allocated a job scrubbing floors. That was it – in the morning on our hands and knees scrubbing floors, break for dinner, and then back on our hands and knees scrubbing floors and then polishing them. Gym twice a week.

But we got down to it. The great thing about Wellingborough was that we got visits every two weeks. Letters really were as many as you wanted, and the visits were for two hours. So things were starting to look up.

Most of the staff in the woodwork shop, the metalwork shop, and the gardeners were all civvies. My job was pressing shirts, hundreds of prison shirts, so I just got stuck in. I got on great with the civvie fellow and that was that.

One day I took my glasses out and Henderson, one of the screws, a very nice screw, asked what I used them for.

'Reading,' I said.

'We're not having that, are we?' he said. They were National Health, and all bent up. 'We'll get you a nice new pair.'

And fair play to him, two days later I was summoned to the office, handcuffed and taken into Wellingborough, to an opticians. They gave me an eye test and told me my new glasses would ready in about a week and would be posted to the borstal.

So, in those two weeks they taught us how to march and salute, and we just fell into line. Then the two weeks ended, and I was sent to work in the laundry.

After dinner every day in the week, each wing would march down to the exercise yard, where Tony and Gaz would be in B-Wing's block, and Harrison in D-Wing's block. Sometimes he would manage to shout a couple of things to me if he could get away with it.

The assistant governor, Connolly, Irish fellow, was a stern, tough fucker; he hadn't got much time for the borstal boys. We used to go to Mass each Sunday in the chapel (the borstal had everything). Connolly, being a Catholic, would bring his family to the chapel, and one Sunday he was walking from the gate to the chapel and someone threw a shit parcel out of the window. He and his children saw it. He was fuming. He banged up the whole side of the block that could have been responsible until he found out who it was.

We still had the pot in the cell, but the cells were lovely; it was your cell, it was your home for the next eight or nine months.

So, I settled in, got on with my job in the laundry, had my visits from Helen. She would get a lift over to Wellingborough with my mate, John Barnacle, for whom I had found a job driving for a fridge company. There were a lot of visits, a lot of driving time spent in each other's company. Once my Mam came to see me with Helen; I loved that visit.

'It's a beautiful place,' Mam said.

'It is, Mam,' I said, 'compared to the Scrubs.'

I had some great visits while I was there.

There was a nice atmosphere during visits. Families would come and they were offered tea and biscuits. But after a visit I was really choked, quiet, and we would queue to be taken back to the wings, to my cell.

May, June, July. I was going to be seventeen soon, and Helen sent a big parcel in for my birthday containing chocolate, sweets and biscuits, which was a lovely treat.

One day I was sitting at the dinner table with the three lads and they had never heard of the word 'chewy'.

'What do you mean, chewy? You mean gum.'

'No, chewy.'

We weren't allowed chewy, but they let me have the parcel from Helen.

I was down the laundry, ironing the shirts. There was a bit of a fiddle going – if someone was due a visit and they wanted to look their best they'd ask you if you could starch the collar and cuffs of their shirt. The going rate was a couple of smokes. The currency was the same as at the Scrubs – Mars bars and tobacco. I was comfortable with my regular wages. Whatever I bought, half an ounce of tobacco, I managed to make it last the week.

Summer came and we would play football and baseball, like rounders, an American thing, in the exercise yard.

Paul Thorne and Terry Green had arrived by now after doing their month to six weeks at the Scrubs, and they got allocated to C-Wing with me, which was good.

The rest of the lads in C-Wing were pretty good. Everyone sort of got on with one another; to be fair, everyone just wanted to do their time and get out.

There was still a lot of tension with the black guys. Haywood, I remember, was just off the wall. He had a proper chip on his shoulder.

But there wasn't a lot of trouble – the odd fight and that was it. The screws would break the fight up, and the parties would be sent down to solitary confinement. The governor would come and sentence them to whatever he thought fit and that was that.

We used to have a volunteer who came to see the Catholic boys every Wednesday. He was a young guy, a mad City fan, and he would chat to us about what was happening in the city.

We used to have an association after work, after tea. It was pretty good. You'd play pool, draughts, chess, watch the telly; everyone seemed to get on with each other. That was where I realised that there was one thing I was really good at – draughts. I used to play all the good players. We played for tobacco, and I ended up winning the Christmas Champion Draughts Player at Wellingborough Borstal in 1971. That's my claim to fame. I'm still a pretty good draughts player now.

We plodded on; the months went by. They wanted someone to work in the Stores, which was a better job, so I went there to work for a small, balding fellow, a civvie. On Fridays all the inmates would come and hand in their dirty clothes and I would give them fresh packs, so I got to see everybody in the borstal. I was recommended for that job by the laundry, and I did enjoy it. We got the pick of the best uniforms in the Stores, and if someone wanted an extra shirt you'd slip them one.

I'd got up to brown tie by then and the next tie would be discharge. We had a bit more freedom by then, and the screws respected us. They were all civvies, wearing civilian clothes. A lot of them were ex-army guys, or RAF. There weren't any horrible ones; they were all pretty good. Their job was to try and help us get ready for when we got out.

We were measured up for a tailor-made suit for when we got out, so we left with a good set of clothes. Things were getting easier and I was making the most of it. There was no bother, in fact I was loving it. My best mate in there was Michael Hickey from St Neots. Me and him sort of ran everything.

I remember coming in from work around November time. Terry Green had got this fat Garratt lad from Wellingborough (a local lad doing borstal), and he was threatening to throw darts at him.

I said, 'What's happening, Greeney?'

He said, 'I'm threatening him for the duff, the pudding, for tomorrow.' The puddings in the borstal were absolutely gorgeous.

I pulled Garratt away and Greeney made a big thing of licking the point of the dart and aiming it at Garratt. But when he threw the dart it missed Garratt and went straight in my leg, and he laughed. So I gave him a belt and we started fighting. Well, he still had the two other darts in his hand and he was stabbing me with them!

Anyway, we got broken up and sent down to the block. Everything was different there; it was a different regime. Everything was double time. If you were speaking to a screw you'd be marching on the spot. Anyway, we saw the governor the next day; my record until then was spotless. The governor said, 'We know your situation at home and you don't want to be losing any time, do you?'

I replied, 'No, sir.'

He said, 'I will sentence you to a week in the block,' which I settled for.

It was tough. I'd get up in the morning, put my furniture outside and sit there with a book and a table. The meals were basic and minimal.

They let us out on Christmas Eve, and when I went back on the wing Hickey was there and he handed me a cigar. He said, 'Merry Christmas, Sully.'

I'd got six weeks left to do. It was a good Christmas – I remember it well.

One day I was summoned to the governor's office, and Matron had told me, very gently, that I'd had a Dear John letter. They watched as I took it in, wondering how I'd react. I just stood there. It all made sense, in hindsight.

What I hadn't bargained on was John Barnacle's betrayal. Long before any of this trouble came to court, I'd confided in him that when I heard Helen was in labour, I was with a girl called Jane who worked at NatWest Bank. My mam was in Ireland visiting Sheila O'Connor, so I had taken her back to our house. It wasn't exactly saintly behaviour, I grant you, but the way John Barnacle must have spun it for Helen, well, I can imagine how he'd paint me. So she broke it off, and John Barnacle was standing by, poised and ready to pounce.

Matron waited, then quietly suggested, 'You're going to look back on this one day, and think, "Aren't I the lucky one."' I now totally agree, but it took a long while to get that perspective on things.

They were a bit worried at the borstal, thinking that I might do a runner, so they kept an eye on me. I was in a trusted position and when someone in that position received bad news, a death in the family, break up of a relationship, that was what they did. But I just got on with it.

I was choked, obviously, but that was it. The visits stopped; the letters stopped. Mary still wrote to me; Mam still wrote to me. I even got a letter from my brother John, the one and only.

For a second time I was called into the governor's office, again with Matron. 'Your sister's had a baby.' Mary hadn't come to court to see me sent down because she'd been in the unmarried mothers' home in Derby. Mary had a daughter, Bonnie, fathered by some runaway who was into drugs, David, I think his name was. He was gone by the time I got out of borstal. Mam became her full-time babysitter. They came to see me, but the baby was only two or three months old.

My release date was 18 February 1972, and three weeks before that I'd got home leave for a week. The time dragged then. I just needed to get out and see what was happening. Thanks to the likes of Hickey, I managed to get by.

The day came for the week of home leave. I was told that I'd be getting the train to Leicester from Wellingborough. I'd be arriving in Leicester between three-thirty and four o'clock and I was to go straight to my probation officer, Miss Horner, and she was going to take me to see Helen and the baby. And that's what she did.

The atmosphere was tricky. Helen's mum and dad were there. But it was okay.

I couldn't wait to go home and to see my family, so Miss Horner dropped me off; she was great. Mam kissed and hugged me, and Mary did the same. Mary slipped me a pound and said, 'There you are, have a drink on me.' That might not seem like much, but it was back then.

Gary Bakewell knocked on the door. He'd been out a couple of months, and we went into town. I was getting myself ready. I was going to have my first pint in eleven months. Gary had got no money, surprise, surprise. There was a good gang waiting for me in the George in town. It was my night of freedom. I remember someone coming up behind me, putting their hands over my eyes and kissing me. I thought it might have been Helen. But no, it was Cathy Murphy, who was going out with Tony Elliott.

During my home leave, Mam was going on about the television licence one day at the bus stop. I had a bank book with £12 in it. I told Mam that it was what I was saving to get married. The television licence was £6 and the Post Office was only across the road. So we went into the Post Office and I paid for the television licence. Mam was over the moon; life at home would have been pretty grim without that telly.

When I walked into our sitting room, I saw a young woman changing a baby boy's nappy on the floor. I thought it was my son, Lee. 'This is Ann,' my sister announced. 'We were in the unmarried mothers' home together.' They had become best friends, and we'd be seeing a lot of Ann over the next few years.

I went back to Wellingborough Borstal and served out the remaining two weeks of my sentence and was discharged on 18 February 1972. I went to reception on discharge day and put on the suit they'd had made for me. I had already worn it because we had to wear them on home leave and come back in them.

A lot of people never came back from their home leave, even though they only had two more weeks to do. Paddy Byrnes from Scotland never came back. But then they were on the run again. And when they did catch them and bring them back, they got time added to their sentence.

One Irish kid I remember, Lynch, was on the run from an Irish borstal. He'd served his time here, and when he was released, the Irish police gate arrested him and took him back to Ireland.

Anyway, I was on the train after an early start; they wanted you out of the way so they could get ready for the new intakes. I was free!

The next day I went up to see my old boss Keith Hunt at the refrigeration firm Folpack. The boss said, 'When do you want to start?'

I said, 'As soon as possible.'

I was finished with borstal. I was on licence for the remainder of the two years, thirteen months it was, so I had to keep my nose clean.

I had to see my probation officer, and when my two years were up I would be free altogether.

When I came out, my days of football thuggery were over. I was only seventeen. Other things were a bit more important, and I lost interest in Leicester City. I always kept an eye out as to how they got on, but it was time to move on. I still kept in touch with the lads.

That was the end of my 'borstal days'. Some great times, some sad times, but overall, I think it did me the world of good.

PART THREE

Chapter Twenty-Five

Getting Sorted

Towards the end of 1972, I organised myself a solicitor, having spotted a little firm in Wycliff Street in Leicester. I made an appointment and met the guy there – a young fellow. I told him my situation, didn't hold anything back, and he said, 'Well, it's looking a bit bleak, you know. No chance you're going to get custody or anything like that, and you never will. We'll apply to see what we can get. Maybe, you know, a half-day.' Anyway, the day we came to court, their solicitor rubbished me left and right. He went on for about twenty minutes. Then it was my turn to talk.

I stood up and said to the judge, 'I've been here twenty minutes answering questions, and I've managed to do it without swearing. I think I can conduct myself.'

The judge went into his chambers. When he returned, he said, 'You will be granted an hour a month in the property of Mr and Mrs Aplas [Helen's mum and dad].'

My solicitor said, 'That's what we'll work on.'

The first appointment was at two o'clock on a Saturday afternoon and I sat there for a whole hour. Helen's mum and dad were there,

Barnacle was there, and they were chatting to each other, making each other tea, but they didn't offer me one. Lee was a little toddler, crawling. He came and had a look at me and then just carried on playing; it was the longest hour of my life. Anyway, I got through it. The same thing happened the next month, and by the third month Barnacle was making snidey remarks. I put up with it as long as I could, but in the end I got up, grabbed hold of him, and gave him a good beating. Eddie, Helen's dad, tried to break it up, but I wasn't having it. Anyway, that was that. They were happy as Larry because I'd played into their hands. Within a week, a letter arrived stating I was forbidden to go anywhere near the premises. Helen married Barnacle and he adopted Lee. They later went on to have a daughter. And that was the end of it as far as I was concerned with Lee.

Once I accepted that Helen and Lee were no longer part of my life, I began to feel freer, as if I had a second chance to be a teenager. It felt great. No more hassles.

By the time my eighteenth birthday rolled around, my life had been transformed. I had a lovely time. A few lads joined me in Sloopy's nightclub for a steady evening, no wild nonsense. I was committed to no woman, enjoying my freedom to play the field, had decent clothes on my back and a good job. One of my mates toasted me: 'You're old enough now to smoke, drink, vote and go out in the world, and be a father.' Apart from the voting lark, I'd been doing everything else for years!

I had started taking driving lessons; things felt good. I was still living at home, but John had moved out to live with Mary's friend Ann whom she'd met at the unmarried mothers' home. They rented a house in Highfields on Hart Road and John was acting as a dad to her son Neil. Ann had come home one day to find her previous boyfriend in bed with another woman, so John came over, ran him off, and decided moving in with Ann was his way forward.

Mam's house had been tense when he and I were there together. He fancied himself as a bit of a rocker, all long hair and leather, and I was the typical skinhead. We were like chalk and cheese and would often fight good and proper. Since John was not keen on personal hygiene or changing his clothes, when it came time for him to pack up, there was only a small bag of his belongings to take across to Hart Road. He walked down to the end of the road to catch the bus, which was waiting at the terminus. As he sat on the upper deck gazing out the window, he spotted a plume of smoke coming from the direction of Mam's house.

Before he'd even left the neighbourhood, Mam had dragged his stinking mattress out to the side garden and set fire to it. I was there, witnessing the scene, howling with laughter. She let him know quite pointedly, 'There's no coming back.' She'd had her bellyful of forcing him into his weekly bath and holding his underwear out at arm's length to finally give it a wash. Ann had no idea what she was letting herself in for. Ann got pregnant with John. Lo and behold, when the baby was due, she decided to have it in Nottingham. When she was due, me and John borrowed a car off Fred at the Longstop and drove to Nottingham – Queen's Medical Centre, where she was having the baby. We got there and the baby had been born – a boy.

John was absolutely over the moon. He'd got a son. He said we'll call him John – Jonny. We used to joke that he would end up a Nottingham Forest fan.

We came back to Leicester and John changed the tradition. When a man has his first son, he usually buys the drinks for everyone and dishes out cigars. John turned that one around. He expected everyone to buy him drinks and hand him cigars, which they did. Everybody was happy for him. The baby came home; John and Ann had got a house in Highfields on Berners Street. After a few months, Ann went back to work. Just as today, childminders were very expensive, so John decided that he would look after the baby.

One day I went to visit him. He was lying across the floor with the television and the gas fire on, making toast by holding the bread to the fire with a fork. He had a bowl of butter by his side too. And at the same time he was rocking the baby with his foot in a bouncy chair. I said, 'What are you fucking doing, John?'

He said, What's it look like?'

I said, Why don't you do the toast under the grill?'

It was laziness!

As time passed it wasn't working with Ann, poor thing. She was working all hours. The relationship broke up. John said when anyone asked, 'Well, I tried married life.' Although he had never got married. 'I tried it, and I didn't like it. I want to be a free man.'

John was always a character. I am amazed how he got through life without reading, never even agreeing to have a secret pair of glasses. His eyesight was as poor as mine, but his ear for music was second to none. He had his favourite LPs and knew his music inside out. At this time he was a labourer, working on the roads for the city. He and his friends would meet up on a Friday night after work.

Every Saturday night, my friends and I would get dressed up in suits and ties and take pride in looking smart. I'd lost interest in Leicester City football by then. The thought of getting into fights at away games had lost its appeal.

A gang of us used to meet up at the George at the Clocktower – Rob Smith and his Vicky, a hairdresser; Nick Loxley; the Bakewell brothers, and me with Vicky's mate, Jane, whom I was courting at the time. The George was the in place to be. There was tacit social segregation: half of the room was our gang, and the other half was black. It wasn't tense, that's just the way it was. Bill Dean, known as Dixie, was a hefty mixed-race bouncer. He's still a good friend of mine. Tony Elliot was there too; he neither drank nor smoked. He was shrewd; by then he had his own garage and was very much on an even keel.

Terry Franklin, 'the Fox', was a regular and mixed race like Dixie. Terry and his mate Steady were shoplifters. Terry was into drugs and drink and poor Steady was not exactly the full shilling. Everyone tried when they came out of prison for a 'clean, fresh start', but it was hard to achieve. Much easier to slot back with old friends and familiar ways. Lots of guys from the Scrubs passed through my social world. Fine, upstanding role models were in short supply.

Mary was not working. I used to tell her off and try to straighten her out, but it fell on deaf ears. She seemed to be attracted to the wrong sort of man. Her choices went from bad to worse. My sister could hold her liquor, and match her brothers drink for drink. She preferred life on the darker, wilder side. Her daughter was largely left to Mam. Little Bonnie became very close to her grandmother, and a lasting bond developed. Mary craved excitement. She had no patience in playing the long game for delayed gratification. Perhaps she felt, after the struggles our family had endured, that she was 'owed' some pleasure and self-indulgence and was determined to grab it at every opportunity. There was an anger deep inside her, a resentment of what life had thrown at her, that burst out in rebukes to her teachers and, later, a refusal to engage with the system of education or the world of work. Look what being good had ever done for her mother – trapped on the poverty line in dead-end cleaning jobs, abandoned by a useless husband. *If life dumped on you, don't waste time trying to change the inevitable. It's hopeless. Grab your pleasures when and where you can.*

She never listened to a word I said to persuade her otherwise.

As far as my work was concerned, things were going great. My boss, Keith, and I had a few decent perks along the way. We delivered the freezers for the supplier right enough, but if any extra fitting was required, a spot of electrics, that cash was ours. I wanted to upgrade my skills and was sent to the distribution centre to be taught how to repair freezers. It was located at the top of Saffron Lane and took me two buses to get there. I was able to sell on any freezers that were condemned, another little earner. There may have been two a week and my savings were adding up. I opened a bank account. I was earning about £20 a week on top of my wages. I was able to buy Mam her first fridge. Up until then she'd still been keeping the milk cool in a bucket of cold water. The best bonus was that after about two and a half years I was a qualified engineer.

Mary took up with Tony Bakewell. Terry was the eldest of the three brothers; we didn't see much of him. Tony was the middle brother, a big fellow, over six foot. Gary was the youngest brother, the same age as me, and I was best man for him a few years later when he married Vicky. His father, Harry, was quite a Leicester character, and well known throughout the city. Tony's mother, Vera, worked to keep the household afloat. She had to put up with a lot. I remember Tony telling me they used to have a slot TV, coin operated. Once, the two lads were short of cash and broke into it. Inside, they found a note: 'Beat you to it – Dad.'

Tony was in Welford jail, serving two-thirds of an eighteen-month sentence. Mary and Tony decided to get married, and I was asked to be best man. I thought marriage might straighten her out, settle her down. Wouldn't do Tony any harm either, if he took it seriously. The Catholic priest at Holy Cross was chaplain to the prison and arranged everything. Tony was going to be allowed out for the day, with a couple of prison guards as escorts.

I made my own way to the church. Mary was dressed smartly, but not in full bridal gear. A mate of mine, John Williams, was a subcontracted driver for the fridge firm. He had an E-Type Jag and kindly picked Mary up and drove her to the church in style. I was sitting on the front bench on the groom's side, waiting for the guards to un-cuff Tony so he could sit beside me. When he finally arrived, I slipped him a hip flask of whiskey. Not exactly stag night revelry, but better than nothing. A little Dutch courage never hurt anyone.

After the ceremony, the guards let them take a few photos, then whisked him back around the corner to his Welford Road cell. I splashed out on a big party back at Mam's for Mary. It was open house, and proved to be the biggest party Mowmacre Hill had ever seen. By then all the anti-Irish bigotry had faded into ancient history. The party went on for ages. I slipped into town for a quiet drink or three with Nick Loxley, who was now our John's lodger over in Hart Road.

Enforced separation is never a good start for a marriage. Prison gossip and jibes don't help either. Tony became jealous. He had always been selfish, needy, some might call it, but so was Mary. She needed someone to pay her attention. While Tony was still in prison she started seeing David Holland, who was into drugs. Tony had a liking for heavy drinking, which Mary could easily match, but David was a different level of beast. He used to shake down junkies to take their dole money off them. He was a bouncer at a top club in town, so a big, beefy bloke used to getting his own way.

It was my uncomfortable task to collect Tony from Welford Road on the morning of his release. It was 7.30 in the morning. Pouring rain. It was like a scene from an old black and white gangster film. The small door in the big gates opened and out came Tony. Under one arm he was carrying a wooden rocking horse that he said he had made for Bonnie.

'Where's Mary?' He looked stunned. He read the situation before I had time to explain. After a pause I told him straight. 'She's living with Dave Holland in one of his flats.'

Bonnie was with Mam, and Mary would come over to visit her when she was right-side up. Holland got her into drugs as well as drink, so visits were irregular. Mam had to stand by helpless as Mary's life spiralled out of control. There was one thing she could do for Mary, though. Since Mary and Tony had never had time to be together after the ceremony, Mam set the wheels in motion to get that paper marriage annulled.

I used to play with Bonnie when I got home from work. She was a lovely child, but she worried me. The little girl was chatting while playing with me when she was no more than five, and started miming an action on her ankle. It took a minute or two to grasp what she was pretending to do: inject a needle as she must have seen her mother do. Mam had no idea Bonnie would have been exposed to that side of Mary's life.

In time, Mary moved into a council house, pregnant with Dave's child. She had a boy, Paddy. Dave was by then disappearing at all hours. He was beating her up.

I came home one Friday night from town on the bus and Mam told me about Mary. Mary had been on the phone to her in tears. He'd given her another beating. I immediately drove over in the van to fetch her. Dave came for me with a broken milk bottle. He was a mountain of a man, and not one I'd choose to mess with. I screamed at Mary to get into the van. Once she was safe, I tackled the bully, giving him a taste of his own medicine. 'You beat up my sister, you have me to deal with.'

On the drive back to Mam's, I told her she'd better forget him. She was shaking and grateful for her rescue, agreeing with me, but it didn't last long. Mam overheard her on the phone the very next morning, all sweetness, making up to Dave.

Eventually Dave received a good long prison sentence. I took Mary to visit him once. Only once. 'I'm not going to hang around for him,' she told me. Holland was going to meet the same fate as Tony Bakewell. It couldn't have happened to a more deserving guy.

Pam, Tim, Mam, John and Johnny on John's 40th

Chapter Twenty-Six

The Long Stop

In the spring of 1973 a new pub opened up across the street from our usual, the George. There had been mounting tension between black and white and, as the clientele in the George had always been mixed, it was no longer a comfortable place to hang out. The Cricketer's Arms had been a typical town-centre pub, very smoky with a stained ceiling. It had been quite popular with Irish navvies. Although owned by the same M&B brewery, it had the advantage of a recent refurbishment, impressive with its red carpet, flock wallpaper and panelling, and was renamed the Long Stop. It lacked a backyard and there was only one way in, however. This may have been a downside for the punters but was a real bonus for the police.

The Long Stop also had the latest attractions: a big pool table and a good jukebox. The gaffer, Fred, was an ex-copper from Coventry, a nice fellow. A lot of people were leaving the George to head across the street. It was beginning to get a right good craic in there. There was a wider social mix. I remember Ralph McDonald was a great pool player. A couple of my friends from school were there: Chris Griffin and John Bone. John had been in my sister's year and he became a barman there. After I bought my first drink, he'd see to it I never paid for another that night. I could enjoy a whole night out for only a couple of quid. John was a trusted employee and would take over when Fred was on holiday. He understood the various dodges and fiddles that went with the job, such as which punters wouldn't spot watered-down beer, how the cigarettes were sourced and priced. Fred knew everything would be as he left it when John was in charge.

One Friday night in 1973, I was down the Long Stop early on. Things were good. Sonny Hill, the son of the rag 'n' bone man on Stocking Farm, was in. He was into drugs and was one of the hardest men walking the town. He could fight like a proper gipsy and he wasn't scared of anything. We were having a craic. Somebody came in and said, 'There's a load of Hells Angels over in the Churchill, celebrating something.' So Sonny decided he was going to go over and get his colours, which referred to the emblem the Hells Angels have on their back.

We said, 'Sonny, don't! Leave it, leave it. These ain't mugs. These aren't your run-of-the mill idiots.' Anyways, it was too late, he had run out of the door. We went to make sure he was okay. When we got to the Churchill, we could hear the noise and the music coming from downstairs. We went down the stairs, and it was packed with Hells Angels celebrating. We went to the bar to get a drink.

Sonny was in the middle of a group of Hells Angels waving his arms around. They were ignoring him. And then he made a lunge at one of the jackets and said, 'I want this jacket.' Well, it all kicked off and went up in the air. I went over to get Sonny out. The next thing I knew, I was attacked. The place was in uproar. When I managed to get to my senses, I was lying on the floor and my head was bleeding. The only people there were the bar staff, the barmaid and the manager.

'Are you OK?' they said.

'Yeah, yeah, I think so, yeah. Sound.'

They said, 'Stay where you are. Your head's bleeding. You've been hit with a broken bottle.'

I said, 'I'll be all right, I'll be all right.'

They bandaged my head but I felt the blood coming from my side. They said, 'My God, we've got an ambulance on the way. It looks like you've been stabbed.'

The ambulance crew arrived. They patched my head up, patched my side up, and said, 'You're going to have to go down to Casualty. We'll take you down there, get you stitched up.'

I remember being there, lying on the trolley in the cubicle. The nurses and doctors came in and said, 'You've been stabbed with an instrument. We've put five stitches in your head and four inches of stitches in your side. But now we're going to give you some injections.'

I said, 'Yeah, no worries.'

They turned me on my side and gave me a needle, no problem. Then they said, 'This one's going to hurt a bit more. It's a tetanus jab.'

I hadn't had one since I was a kid. And my God, the pain. I jumped and hit the wall and knocked myself out. When I came round they said, 'You're OK, just dazed.' And I broke wind. Oh, that was embarrassing. I was able to walk, so I said, 'I'll sort myself out,' and I left the hospital.

A couple of the lads were there and they gave me a lift home. When I got in the house I found John had his nose broken in town. He was gawking at the mirror at his swollen nose. What an atmosphere. Mam was crying her eyes out. 'Jesus Christ almighty tonight. What's it going to be next? Stabbings and broken noses. My God,' she said. I crawled up to bed that night. Got up on Saturday morning and went down town.

I had to get the stitches taken out a week later. I went to the surgery on Parker Drive. The nurse said, 'We can't take the stitches out, they've gone septic. I'll get you some penicillin. Take these and come back in three days.'

I went over to Timothy White's, a chemist on the clock tower, and got the tablets, and the label said one three times a day. I thought, well, it's seven thirty in the evening, I better take the three tablets and I've done day one. Twenty minutes later, I could not stop laughing, and people were asking what was the matter. I said I didn't know. But it must have been the penicillin. It was the only time in my life I had any side effects from drugs. But I thought, is that what taking drugs does? It makes you happy? Anyway, I went back three days later and they took the stitches out, so it was all back to normal.

It was a new fad for girls in a group to go on a pub crawl. They'd try the various local spots out and if the atmosphere suited them, if it was lively enough, they might hang on and stay all night. With the Long Stop's central location, this venue now had a lot of people coming and going throughout an evening, people I wouldn't previously have had the chance to meet.

What changed my life around? A bit of flashy carpet and a pool table? Feeling under pressure in the old George? It's the small choices one makes almost unconsciously that can make all the difference.

I was seeing no one at the time. I'd not long finished with Julie Wright, whose dad owned a butcher's shop. It had fizzled out naturally. The Long Stop had become my home from home every Thursday, Friday and Saturday.

It was still quite chilly in the evenings. I spotted a pair of girls coming in, both very good looking. One of them was extra special, and I couldn't take my eyes off her. She had her dark hair pinned up, and her pale complexion was framed by the fur collar of her jacket. There was a spark to this one, intelligent eyes. She carried herself with assurance. She wasn't loud, silly or too tipsy like others that dropped in. In fact, as I watched her, she didn't seem much of a drinker at all. She didn't flaunt herself in a short skirt, but wore well-chosen, flattering trousers. Good taste. She was gorgeous. I had to speak to her.

'Can I buy you a drink?'

As if to test my interest, after a bit of coaxing, she replied, 'I'll have a whiskey and dry.' I brought her a double. *She might be impressed.* It was worth a gamble – by that time of night, thanks to John, I wasn't paying. We chatted briefly, and then she was off. As she left, I teased her, 'You owe me a drink.' She laughed and slipped out the door. I didn't even know her name.

About a month later I bumped into her again, this time in the George. I found out my mystery woman was Pam Carter. She worked in the market on Lineker's family stall. Her best friend and pub companion was Angela (Angie) McGlinchy. She had three brothers and two sisters. I was still working on the wagons delivering fridges with Speedy Williams in my day job, and a few days later, when we had time on our hands, I suggested we drive down to the market to see if Pam was on the stall. I saw her. She waved and tossed me an apple. *That's a good sign,* I thought.

Pam, for her part, was always a cute girl. She used to go out at the weekend with her trusted best friend, and was wary of strangers trying to chat her up. She thought I was a bit of a bruiser at first and kept me at arm's length. That running joke, 'You owe me a drink', was getting tiresome. She decided to buy me half a pint to shut me up. I was persistent; she gave me that.

Over the next few weeks, I kept seeing her out with Angie. I did my best to be charming and persuasive, but she kept refusing to go out with me. 'I'm too busy,' she'd always tell me. Eventually she gave in. I was able to take her out for a drink or two on Sunday nights because the market was closed on Mondays. I had yet to pass my driving test, so at the end of the evening I'd walk her to the bus stop and Pam would head off to her home in Goodwood and I'd return across town to Mowmacre Hill. Because of the transport hassles we could only ever meet in the centre of town. That was probably a blessing in disguise. Had her family met me and known my history from the outset, I probably wouldn't have stood a chance. By the time we did finally meet, Pam had had time to reassure her mam and dad that there was more to me than a chequered past.

We went on several dates. One was to see the latest film, *The Exorcist*. Pam and her family had no religion, but she knew I was Catholic. I found the movie much more upsetting than she did. I swore I'd bent down in some scenes to tie a loose shoelace. Pam spotted this big, tough bruiser of a guy was actually wearing slip-ons. The more we got to know one another, the more she was certain there was more to this man than rough streets.

On each of these dates, the evening would be pleasant, we would get along fine. When it came time to say goodnight, however, there were no kisses. No fumblings. No trying it on. She was puzzled. *What's up with this guy?* She hadn't expected this rough diamond from the wrong end of town to be such a gentleman. It unsettled her.

It was during this time that I was desperate to learn to drive, to gain my own set of wheels and be done with the buses getting in the way of my courting. I had been having lessons. It was an open secret that I was a good driver. My boss at the fridge warehouse used to leave me in charge when he was away. I used to take one of the wagons home at the end of the day. I wouldn't go out in it at night, mind you. Mam was having kittens, worrying that I'd be caught driving without a licence.

Friday 13 December was my test day, out on Narborough Road facing the Huntsman pub. I met my examiner as scheduled and according to plan he asked me to read a number plate at a distance. I complained the car he chose was too far away. He selected a second. Again, I protested the distance. He was getting exasperated, and I was not helping my chances. He stomped into the office, returning with a measuring tape. We finally agreed on a car; I read it accurately.

He was not in a good mood and was very strict in his manner. As we came round Granby Halls I was spotted by Graham Tebbit and Sonny Hill, who were known junkies. They clocked my situation and shouted out taunts, trying to put me off. My choice of acquaintances did nothing to enhance the examiner's opinion of me. It came to reversing around a corner. I unwisely confessed, 'This is one of my weak points.'

He solemnly grumbled, 'I don't want to be knowing that.'

After all the hassle I'd put him through, I was convinced I'd failed, but the fellow passed me in spite of my awkward behaviour and dodgy mates.

That Friday it snowed heavily. I returned to work – it was payday. In the normal run of things we'd head off at lunch to a pub round the corner for a few beers. This Friday I had something to celebrate, so I was enjoying myself. Then the gaffer found me and told me his wife was stuck in the snow. Could I, as a now legal driver, drop his kids back at school? I was thrown in at the deep end, driving in a blizzard, over the limit. I don't think I have ever concentrated so hard and been as tense as I was on that first memorable journey.

With a little loan from a friend I managed to buy my first car, a rather flash Zephyr Zodiac, from my workmate Speedy Williams. I rang Pam. 'I've bought a car!' She was delighted. I drove into town to collect her. As we walked towards it, I tricked her into thinking it was the oldest banger in the street, a real wreck. She tried to be polite about it, but when I then showed her my Zephyr, she was suitably impressed.

One day, as I was dropping Pam home, I was able to meet her family without any fuss. I saw her mum approaching the car and stepped out to introduce myself. 'Hello, Mrs Carter. I'm Tim and I'm very pleased to meet you. I've heard a lot about you.' We shook hands.

She checked me out. 'You Irish? You have the look of the Irish.'

Pam had never brought any of her boyfriends home before. She offered to fix me a meal. It was beans on toast, and she burnt the toast. I wasn't put off. Her mam and dad seemed to hit it off with me immediately, and I spent a lot of time in that house. Pam was their middle daughter. Pam's elder sister, Christine, was already married to another O'Sullivan, Pat, but no relation. They lived at St Matthew's. Pat had been brought up in a children's home, with no particular religious background. He worked in the building trade and he'd never been in any trouble with the law. He and Christine went for typical seaside caravan holidays every July Fortnight. Pam had a younger sister called Denise, who was nine years her junior.

Pam's dad, Dennis, worked for the council. He was a man who lived and died for his family. He was also a non-stop talker. Her mother especially clicked with me, loving me from the start. I always had the gift of reading people well, had Mam's sociability, and have often said I trust people till they go bad. Seems like the Carters decided from the outset that I was a 'good 'un' and accepted me as part of the family. I showed up weekly for family meals, big stews and dumplings, everyone around the table together. It was the family environment I'd never had, and I loved it there. I was learning what was possible.

On Boxing Day 1973 I brought Pam over for tea to meet my family. Pam remembers the house was freezing cold and very sparsely furnished. The only heat was a gas fire in the big lounge. There was an atmosphere when she arrived. Mam and Mary had been in the middle of a row. Pam was wary of Mary from the start. She sensed Mary thought her a snob. The two were like chalk and cheese. But Mam took to Pam straight away. She figured Pam was a good influence on her favourite son and she wanted the relationship to work. The meal itself was quite simple, some ham and a plate of bread. Mam apologised for not thawing out the bread properly.

Given Mam's devout Catholic perspective, Pam was surprised when she encouraged her to stay overnight with me. I brought her up a cup of tea the next morning, followed not long after by more tea and toast from Mam, hoping she'd extend her stay. Pam had no doubt she was warmly welcomed. After the constant runaround Mam was having, trying to deal with John and Mary, Pam was a godsend. Mam's upbringing in the children's home had deprived her of the parental role models that might have taught her how to cope. Being abandoned by her husband meant she'd had no financial or emotional help. Pam saw that I had become the father figure of the household, and had felt responsible from an early age. Mam relied on me a lot to calm things down and sort the family out.

Chapter Twenty-Seven

The Visitor

While Pam and I were courting, I was still living at home, the stranger appeared. It was late at night. I was sprawled out on the settee watching the television when there was a loud knock on the back door. Mam went out to see who it was, and I heard her shocked scream. 'Jesus Christ, what the bloody hell you doing here?' I sat bolt upright, ready for trouble. Two seconds later Mam walked in introducing the huge fellow. 'Tim, this is your father,' and announcing to her long-lost husband, 'this is your son, Timmy.'

As a youngster I had longed for a father. Someone should have led this family, shown us how to turn out right, make something of ourselves. I wanted this longed-for hero to be proud of me, maybe even regret the absent years he'd missed, not watching his brood grow up. Maybe it wasn't too late.

What were his first words to the young man, the son he'd abandoned?

'He's no son of mine, he's the nose of a vulture!'

Mam saw her golden boy stunned. She'd borne her own abandonment stoically over all the years, but her hard-working decent lad didn't deserve to be treated like something the cat dragged in. She no longer felt her husband's insults, that he thought the lad might not be his. It was me she felt for. Now I knew what kind of man my father really was. No more dreaming of a hero. It had been kinder never to mention him. Now I stood facing the nasty, selfish brute my Mam had married. Neither had probably been suited to marriage. Mam had been hampered by her upbringing in the children's home, while Tim Senior was, on the kindest reckoning, a natural-born loner. Being attracted to one another in the fervour of their youth, that dazzle, was not enough to build a life together. Mam had had to do her best to be a mother; Tim Senior didn't know how to be a father.

Why he showed up wasn't so much a mystery as a fantastic coincidence. About a month before, a colleague and I were delivering a big chest freezer to a pub landlord over in Nottingham. We had to haul it up three flights of stairs – no easy task. We were tired out. To be fair, the landlord gave us lunch and started chatting to us. Turned out he was an Irishman who had worked in the mines with a Tim O'Sullivan. He knew he'd married a woman called Kathleen and had three kids. That had to be my dad. Big Tim had been in this very pub only a couple of weeks before. That landlord had no doubt passed on our details.

John, his eldest boy, came home accompanied by Tony Bakewell. Tim Senior was delighted and walked up to Tony and shook his hand, assuming he was his first-born son. John was not impressed and backed off. He wasn't bothered by the whole father–son fiasco. He wasn't interested in forging any relationship with the big man.

Mary, with her tumbling, shoulder-length hair and feisty attitude, did stir some paternal interest in the old fellow. She, like her dad, liked a drink a little too much. He could see she needed help. Mam, the teetotaller, could hardly be expected to manage Mary. He'd sort her out. In time, he did try. Mary went to live with him for a time, but he sent her back. She was a troubled child with problems too deep-set to unravel.

That night, when Tim Senior managed to hurt or insult just about everyone in the household, he announced he needed a lift to Grimsby to be in time for work. I had just started a new job with Total Refrigeration based from home, so I said I would take him. We didn't stop drinking until about one in the morning – the two of us plus John, Mary, Tony Bakewell and Norah.

I had just passed my driving test and was skilled at navigating round Leicester, but had never gone any distance. I had the firm's van out front and gave my father the lift, but it meant I arrived in time for my own job back in Leicester without any sleep. On the four-hour journey I learned a lot about my dad and I started to see him in a different light. When we arrived in Grimsby at the house where he was staying, the work van was there waiting to pick him up. As he left I said to my dad that we must stay in touch and he agreed.

Big Tim hauled in his barbed comments on that journey. Perhaps in the dark, the tensions eased. I decided to give him the benefit of the doubt. I wasn't easily shocked, and I had a sense of what could lie beneath a gruff exterior and was by nature reasonably forgiving. I decided I liked the old man. I knew this would upset Mam – she'd feel I was disloyal. But it wasn't about loyalty. I could care for them both. It wouldn't be easy, but relationships in my family were anything but easy. I'd find a way.

When I started with Total Refrigeration, they put a phone in for us and paid for it, so we didn't have to use Jeff's next door. Jeff was very relieved about that. My dad could never pilot a phone, so he'd always get someone to ring. Anyway, one day he said to me, 'Why don't you come down and bring Pam for the weekend?' He was in Plumstead. I said I'd love to.

I said, 'I'll come down on Friday night, Pam will come on Saturday, and we'll come back on Sunday.' I went down in the van on the Friday night. I knew Aunt Mary, Dad's sister, pretty well, and their son John (Fox). We stayed with Aunt Mary and went out with John. His local was the Lord Derby in Plumstead, next to the train station, and I met his friends there. On Saturday, Pam landed. She managed to get to Plumstead on the train from Leicester and we walked straight to the Lord Derby. Dad finished work about five o'clock, and he joined us. And all I did was drink all night. And the Irish lads were buying Pam whiskey, and she couldn't drink it. I said, 'Tip it on the floor.' I was taking the whiskey, putting it under the table and tipping it out. When I got up to go to the toilet, my shoes were full of whiskey.

That night, Auntie Mary said to Pam, 'You can sleep with Olive.' She was a cousin of mine over from Ireland. She didn't want us to sleep together in the same room. We weren't married, but the old man put his foot down and Pam and me shared a room.

I said I'd be back and Dad said, 'When it came time to leave, I said I'd be back and Dad said, 'Bring your brother with you.'

When I saw John. He said he'd love to go.

So John and I set off on one Friday night for the return visit. Big Tim was working in Kilburn by now, but he said, 'Come down, I'll see you when I finish work.' When we got off at St Pancras, we asked about ten people how we would get to Kilburn.

Anyway, we eventually got to the pub, and the old man came in from work at half past six with five of his navvy mates. John was throwing the drinks down. He'd had about eight or nine pints. I told him to slow down. He said, 'They'll be shouting last orders in a minute, ten o'clock.' But we realised in London they didn't close until eleven, so he was over the moon. God knows how many beers he had.

We all walked back to the digs; apparently, it was an Irish guy's house we were stopping at. There was one camp bed for me and John to share when we got there. They were all sleeping in the same room in beds with a big bucket to piss in. It was horrible and cold. There was a little heater that you had to put a shilling in. We tried to sleep, but I kept getting up in the cold to have a piss in the enamel bucket. This was annoying the others because they had to be up at six the next morning. One of them shouted, 'Jesus Christ, Tim, what sort of son is that, two pints and ten pisses?' It was fucking freezing. The next day they got up at six, had their breakfast and said, 'We'll see you tonight.'

'Fuck this,' I said to John, 'I'm not spending another night in this dump.' So off we went to Aunt Mary's in Plumstead. She welcomed us with open arms and cooked us a beautiful breakfast. John was there, our cousin. We stayed there Saturday night and went to see the old man on Sunday. He finished at dinnertime, so we had a few drinks and headed back to Mam's. And that was John's trip to London. It was nice. We had kept in touch, saw the old man, and met some of his friends.

Pam and I decided that we would go away on holiday. My mate Jack Cockroft and his girlfriend Cathy, who he had been with since schooldays had decided on Yugoslavia. Why there I don't know, but I was game for it. We saved £20 a week, and come July, we were ready. It was all booked. We got the bus to Luton Airport and Pam cried for her mam on the way down.

We got the plane to Pula, which is in Croatia now. Our hotel was pretty basic. In those days, Yugoslavia was a neutral country. We met a great couple from Sheffield, Pete and Marina. Pete worked at Whitbread Brewery. Marina, his girlfriend, had a finger missing after protecting him in a fight in Sheffield. But they were great people. So the six of us made the best of a two-week holiday. The weather was perfect – red hot. We spent all day in the sea and on the beach, and I tried to teach Pam to swim. We bought a lilo and had fun every day.

It was July and the World Cup was on. The final in 1974 was between Germany and Holland, but there were no TVs there. We managed to track one down about thirty miles away in a sort of YMCA hostel, but we had to get there on a bus. We met a Dutch fella. He said, 'Every time Holland score, I will buy you drinks.' Holland managed to score and he got the drinks; in fact the drinks were flowing and we were getting a bit loud. The locals didn't like it. They came over and switched the TV off. We could not understand their language, and they could not understand us. I stood up and put the TV back on. They turned it off again. I put it back on and gave the guy a belt, and the whole place erupted. Tables, chairs, God knows what was thrown around. It eventually calmed down and sorted out, and I put the TV on.

Later, I was in the toilet having a piss. The next thing I knew, two armed coppers, one with a machine gun, and the other with his gun drawn, were shouting at me and pointing, 'Put your hands up.'

I said, 'Hang on, let me finish this piss.' But they weren't having it and threw me against the wall. They dragged us out of the toilets. They had me, Pete from Sheffield, and this Dutch fella. They were talking but we couldn't understand a word.

The manager couldn't understand us either. He just pointed to us and said, 'Trouble, trouble.'

The next thing I knew, they had put us in the back of a black van. They slammed the doors. It was pitch black and a hot day. You couldn't see anything. *Fucking hell, where are we going now? We are in a bit of shit here. This ain't, Skegness*, I thought. The Dutch fellow said, 'I am feeling poorly.' We could hear him but we couldn't see him. We couldn't see anything. Then all of a sudden, he started vomiting. *Fuck me,* I thought, *you better not be sick on me.*

The van eventually stopped. They opened the back doors and signalled us to get out. We were in some kind of prison. The prisoners all had T-shirts on and had numbers tattooed on their arms. It didn't take long to realise that this was the local jail. What had I got myself into now? The Dutch bloke was nearly in tears. Pete from Sheffield was calling for Marina. I didn't know where Jack was. He didn't get nicked. I think he bolted and went back to the hotel. He came with us to watch the game, but he wasn't involved in the other stuff. The guard signalled for me and Pete to get in the front of a van. Some prisoners came out with massive hosepipes. They put the Dutch fella in the back of the van, left the doors open, and they hosed the whole van down with him in it, screaming like a pig. The power of the water would have been horrendous. Anyway, that was that. I don't know what happened to the Dutch fella in the end.

They took us to what seemed like a police station. They couldn't understand us, and we couldn't understand them. But they managed to get someone who could speak rough English. He said, 'You're going to be charged with criminal damage, and you'll be in court tomorrow. Now we are going to take you to your hotel and get your passports.'

They took me and Pete back to the hotel. I got out of the van in handcuffs. Pam and the rest of the guests were all staring and looking. Then I heard, 'Oh my God, I think that's Timmy O'Sullivan.' I looked over there was Mrs Woods, my old History teacher. She looked at me handcuffed to the police officer and said, 'I knew you'd never do any good, O'Sullivan.'

The passports were handed over to the police. They uncuffed us and told us to be at court the next day at ten o'clock. In the meantime, some German guys who had been watching the game with us approached us and said, 'We saw everything. It wasn't your fault, they started on you. We will come to court and bear witness to this.' It was such a relief. Brilliant. They said they had a rented car and would take us to court.

The next day we were at court; I was wearing a suit and tie. The Germans could speak Yugoslavian, and they explained everything to the judge, who was wearing a Fred Perry shirt and jeans. You would have thought he was one of the lads. He said, 'I'm going to inspect the damage that has been caused, and I will be round to your hotel tonight to sentence you.'

We went back to the hotel and thanked the Germans. They said they would be at the hotel that night to help us understand. We had a few drinks – it was my birthday, 8 July 1974; I was twenty. I was relieved we were out and having a drink.

The judge turned up later. He was a great guy. In the end, he said he'd had a look and spoken to the German tourists who gave their view of what had happened. He said he was willing to fine us a certain amount of dinars, about £25 back then. It was a hefty fine. He said, 'I warn you, this sort of behaviour is not tolerated in Yugoslavia. You would normally receive six months' detention. If you're in any trouble between now and when you leave in a week, that's where you'll be going.' He was very firm, and then he had a few pints with us. We paid the money, and that was it. Fair play. Time to celebrate.

A couple of days earlier, a couple who were going back home had given us a bottle of champagne because they weren't going to have time to drink it. So out came the bottle of champagne to celebrate my birthday. I shook it up and popped the cork. It flew right across the road and hit a German woman in the neck. I just thought, *Here we go.* But it was sorted out. We managed to keep our heads out of trouble. We didn't go near any more televisions.

We landed at Luton in the pouring rain. It had rained every day in July Fortnight, but we looked well. We were tanned. At Luton airport, Pam said jokingly to me, 'Thank you for a good holiday. I'll see you around.' I thought, *Cheeky bitch.* We realised then, after spending two weeks together, that we couldn't just go back to Sunday nights at Mam's house. We would look for our own place.

One Saturday morning, me and John popped into the Tudor Rose on our way into town. We thought we would have a couple. When we walked in, everything went dead quiet. We looked around and there were a few of the lads in.

Sonny shouted out, 'I see your mates have been busy.'

I said, 'What are you on about?'

He said, 'Your mates in Birmingham.'

I said, 'I haven't got any fucking mates in Birmingham.'

He said, 'The Irish fuckers that blew up the two pubs.'

That was the first we had heard about the disgusting Birmingham pub bombings that had happened the Friday night before. The atmosphere turned to ice. We ordered our drinks, drank up and left. I said to John, 'Come on, let's fuck off out of here.'

That was me done with the Tudor Rose. We went into town and met all the Irish guys. The atmosphere was terrible. Very quiet. I will never forget that day.

But the outrage, it affected everybody. The attitude of the English was pure anti-Irish. Poor Mam, she went through hell. People put boxes outside her house and phoned her saying there was a bomb in the box.

Not long after that, Gary Bakewell informed me that a house had come up for rent next door but one to him, number 118 Bardolph Street. Gary lived at 122. I went and looked. The landlord, Owen, lived next door. He kept an old veg shop that never sold anything. I think it was a front. But anyway, we did the deal. It was £3 a week rent, £1 on the rent book and £2 cash for him, which we settled for. But it was a right dump. Somebody had died there; she must have been a hundred years old. There was one power point downstairs, none upstairs, one light upstairs, and one light downstairs. So there was a fair bit of work to do – Pam wasn't going to move into some shit hole.

Dennis, Pam's Dad, and I rewired it and I dealt with the plastering. There was no hot water. There was an outside toilet, but it was our toilet. We fitted a water heater in the kitchen, so at least we had hot water to wash with. The day we moved in was Easter Sunday. I had been to Mass and had my dinner with Mam. I'd already packed my clothes. I had the firm's van, which was great.

I gave Mam a hug and a kiss, and I said, 'I'm off then, Mam. You can burn my bed now if you want.'

She said, 'I won't be doing that, Timmy.' She was a bit tearful; I was too. I'd lived for eighteen years on Mowmacre Hill, from the age of two, but that was me done with Mowmacre Hill. I thought I'd be more upset, but I was looking forward to the future. I kissed Mam again and said, 'I'll see you in the week.'

And as I drove out of Mowmacre Hill I wasn't looking back. I went up to pick Pam up. In those days, there were no shops open on Easter Sunday, just newsagents. But the garage on Uppingham Road had opened a shop. This was a new thing; garages opened mini-shops where you could get basics: bread, sugar and milk. Barbara took us there, and we bought our first basic groceries. We dropped Barbara back at home, and then Pam and I headed to Bardolph Street. We brought our cases in. Pam looked around and started crying; she wanted her mam already.

Gary Bakewell was next door but one, Tony Bakewell was on Martin Street, the next street, and John was lodging with Tony. Tony had a pickup, and they went out every day scrapping – picking up scrap, earning a couple of quid. Bairdy lived over a shop in Catherine Street at the end of our street with Lavern. Nige Redway was in the next street and Jack Cockroft was only around the corner in Dorset Street, so there was a good bunch of us down there and, you know, we settled in. That was our home.

On Pam's twenty-first birthday, 22 January 1975, I organised a nice meal in a Greek restaurant on Humberston Gate. During the meal I officially proposed to her with an engagement ring.

Pam used to meet up with Mam every week down at the Corn Exchange for drinks. Mam always just had orange juice. Then Pam would slip back to Mam's for a bath. It's a measure of how well the Carters thought of me that when we found this place, it was Pam's dad who did the place up and put in a new kitchen.

Pam felt there was a real community atmosphere on Bardolph Street. Tony Sibson lived just across the road with his mam and dad, Keith and Cath; they were sound, you would always get a sub from Keith. Tony was sixteen at the time and would later become a middleweight Commonwealth and European champion boxer. He was a three-time world title challenger, fighting during the 70s and 80s.

Pam and I came from different worlds. We didn't rush into this relationship. We courted a good while, tried going away together, and then moved in together for about three and a half years.

Pam carried on working at Leicester market for Lineker's Fruit and Veg, and later became manageress of Super Towels. She was well respected by the owner with whom she worked for over twenty-five years. In that time she helped him open a number of other branches.

We had a rhythm to our lives when we lived on Bardolph Street. Weekends were centred around visiting Mam, getting the chance of a bath, and hitting the town for a bit of a social life. I went out with the lads Friday nights, and as soon as the pubs opened again on Saturday morning. Pam worked all day Saturdays, which was a busy day, so she preferred a quiet night Fridays.

I was drinking heavily back then. I was out of order. When the pubs shut at 2.30 in the afternoon, we'd head off to drinking clubs in the Highfields area, like the John F. Kennedy or the Hema, until pubs reopened at 5.00 p.m. There was a good mix of lads, mostly Irish. I could well have been drinking for twelve hours straight. That was my norm, every weekend. Like I say, I was out of order.

One weekend evening in the winter of 1976, a Dublin fella called Mick Malone and I decided to try out a new trendy wine bar, the French Revolution. We were refused entry by both the boss and his manager. We kicked off. I wrenched the door open, attacking both men. Malone smashed the windows in. We fled the scene, but the police caught us out front of the Grand Hotel.

We were arrested and spent a night in Charles Street cells, charged with ABH (Actual Bodily Harm) and Criminal Damage. Malone was already on a suspended sentence, so I pleaded guilty to the window-smashing so he could try his luck pleading not guilty, and only have to serve his suspended time.

Four months later, in February 1977 we were sentenced at the Crown Court (Castle Court). The pub boss's testimony was horrible. I felt he let a strong anti-Irish prejudice seep in, which didn't help.

Malone got six months plus the twelve added on from his suspended sentence; I was given six months.

Like last time, we were initially dropped off at Welford Road for five days. Leicester lads knew me and gave me tobacco, shampoo, and so on to see me through. Then we were shipped off to Stafford prison (an adult, closed facility). I knew some lads there like Rob Smith and Nige Ridgeway, from Mowmacre Hill. They were in for three years; I'd be out in four months.

I made up my mind: I had to change. *This must never happen again.* I was ashamed of myself, and for Mam, who at that time had two of her three children in prison.

My first job there was in a factory making school chairs. We were bussed there every morning. I was on a machine bending metal tubes to form chair legs. Very boring. I managed to transfer to outdoor work (gardening detail). We were digging irrigation trenches to reclaim boggy land. I loved being out in the open air. Pam visited every fortnight and Mam even managed a few visits. My time flew by.

Malone was assigned to the woodwork shop. He managed to pinch wood glue and passed it on to me during our weekly chapel gathering for Sunday Mass. I was able to baron that glue, a precious commodity for all the matchstick hobbyists building model castles. A decent little sideline.

I was released in June 1977, and walked out into a beautiful day, all kitted out in my suit. I slipped across the road to the corner shop to buy a beer and, as was the custom, toasted the lads as the prison coach drove by taking them off to the factory. I caught the bus to the train station. Pam (looking absolutely gorgeous) was waiting to welcome me home as the train pulled into Leicester.

We had a couple of celebratory drinks in town, then made our way back to Bardolph Street. John had been staying with Pam for those few months so she wouldn't be on her own. He knew we'd appreciate some time alone now, so managed to kip elsewhere for a while.

I had a very good employer, who took me straight back. Mary was in Holloway prison during this period. I managed to take Mam to visit her there. Those female prison guards were tough-looking, no-nonsense types. It would be very unwise to cross them, I reckoned.

One day, I got word that Helen and Barnacle had split up and she'd got a house in St Mark's, which was at the bottom of our street. It was on a new estate, next to the Horse and Jockey. I went around to see Lee. We bonded, even though he didn't know who I was. He was about five or six years old and we got to know each other very well. I told Pam about it.

I would have him every Saturday when Pam was working and I took him to football. We went fishing, which he loved. I bought him a rod. We would go out to the quarries in Switherland Woods, which I had fished as a kid – there were big perch in there – fishing on worms for bait. This went on for twelve months. Sometimes I would pick him up on Sunday mornings, and the lads all got to know him. We'd end up in the George on Sunday dinnertime. Pam had met him by then. I had nothing to do with Helen much; I just used to pick him up and drop him off. Then Helen started courting a soldier and my relationship with Lee faded from there. Somebody told me they saw Helen getting married to a soldier in full uniform.

The next thing I heard, he had been stationed in Germany so they were living there. Months later, I heard that Lee was playing up over there, thieving from shops – Helen couldn't control him. They had changed his name to Davidson, the third name he'd been given, and he was only seven or eight years old. It was decided that she would send him back to her mam and dad's. He was shipped back to St

Matthew's. Laura and Eddie took him on and got him settled into Taylor Street school. I had lost touch with him, but I used to make a habit of cutting through St Matthew's on my way home, and hoped I could catch Laura at the bus stop across the road from her house. Eventually, I managed to catch up with her and find out how things were. She said, 'Oh, I'm just going home. Would you come for a cup of tea?' We had a chat and she filled me in about Lee. She said he was alright. Then I didn't hear any more about Lee for some time.

Chapter Twenty-Eight

Settling Down

In about 1977 I was working in Coventry at a supermarket. I had a compressor to fit on a freezer six feet high and three feet wide. I had done it a hundred times before. I had to pick the fridge up, lean it over and tilt it on its side, then take the panels off to get at the compressor. But as I picked the fridge up, I felt something go in my back. And it hurt. I got the job done and went home. My back played up for a couple of days so I went to see the doctor. He was newly qualified by the name of Anroker. He examined me roughly and said, 'You've sprained the muscles in your back. I'll give you some painkillers and put you on the sick.'

I said, 'Wait a minute, I can't afford to be on the sick. And as far as the painkillers go, if you came to me because of a noisy fridge, I wouldn't give you a pair of earplugs, would I?' I didn't bother with the painkillers and just went through it. The pain, some days, was horrendous. I was sleeping on the floor. I wasn't in pain all the time. It would just hit me if I had been standing up for an hour or so. Eventually, I saw Professor Chan.

Chan put me in for a myelogram where they inject a heavy dye into your body and it is then pumped around. When it gets into the brain, there is horrendous pain. I had to spend the night in hospital, and I remember that night well. I couldn't sleep a minute because of the pain.

When I saw Professor Chan two days later, he took one look at the scans and realised how much pain I was in. He said, 'I'll get you in, in a fortnight.' I was taken in to the general hospital. I thought I would be in on Tuesday, have the operation, and maybe come out by Friday. Little did I know how long it would all take; it was never explained. But the operation took seven hours. My testicles were pure black afterwards. I must have been leaned over on a sort of stool. I had a four-inch scar on my back. But it was a success. They took two colossal discs out that were touching my nerves. That was the words they used: colossal. It was a dangerous operation – a laminectomy. If they had made one slip, it would have paralysed me.

I had to sign a waiver stating that they had done their best and if that happened, it wasn't their fault. But all was well after ten days of being bedridden. They got me up on the tenth day and sat me on the side of the bed. By fifteen days, I was up. But I still had another two weeks in hospital. I wasn't cartwheeling around the ward. I was getting by. I was in for a month altogether. When I came out I couldn't work for another three months.

I had a lot of visitors when I was in hospital. It was a bit out of the way, but the lads, Dixie and Terry Franklin used to come up. They brought me – to wind me up – a load of porno magazines. There was a guy on the ward – the major. The nurses thought he was the bee's knees, very upmarket. He hadn't got much time for me. A lot of the other patients were young footballers coming in to have knee operations. I made some good friends there over the month. But the major got on my nerves. He fell asleep one afternoon with a grin on his face. He'd nodded off with the menu for the next day's meals on his bed, ready to be picked up. So I crept over with one of my porno mags open at the middle page and put his menu inside, sticking out of the magazine. When the nurses came by, they saw the magazine wide open. Their attitude towards him changed dramatically. I went over to retrieve the magazine before he woke up. And when he woke he couldn't understand why they were all blanking him. That's the sort of fun and games we had the last couple of weeks there – a good bunch of people.

As the autumn of 1977 drew on, Pam found she was pregnant. We were determined on two things: 1) we were going to be married in a Catholic church before the baby was born, and 2) we were going to buy a house. We were about the last to leave Bardolph Street before it was pulled down.

Father Byrnes, a priest at St Patrick's, took us through the required six pre-marriage sessions. He looked like a young John Denver. When he started the session on children, we assured him we were keen on having a family. In fact, as we'd booked 18 February as the wedding date, we joked we could pencil in a christening for the summer as well. 'Ah, I see.' He smiled nervously, and carried on with his notes.

One day when Pam was over visiting her mother, the pair went out for a walk. There was something Barbara wanted to show her. A whole slew of new-build houses were going up, modest, but with indoor toilets and proper baths. It was clear as day that Pam and I were good together, but our life in Bardolph Street was one step above camping out. We deserved better for all our hard work. Why not move up and try for a mortgage, get something decent?

A mortgage was a huge step. My world had been defined by just scraping by, finding the funds to pay the council rent and whatever was left went on food, heat, and the electrics. I still had vivid memories of the terrifying day we'd all nearly been evicted, with all our pathetic belongings and bits of furniture out on the pavement, until Father O'Sullivan came to our rescue. 'I'm not sure Tim's ready for all that,' Pam confided, 'but I'll float the idea and see what he thinks.'

I didn't have a roadmap of how to get ahead. Mam was clueless about money, and spent what little spare she ever had immediately on her few pleasures, a little betting down the bookie's, a bit of teetotal social life down the pub. My father was a disaster, having made a mess of his life. My older brother could be entertaining as the day was long, but practically allergic to work. Poor Mary never had a clue.

Only the Carters seemed to have managed the knack of being working class, having quite ordinary jobs, and having a lovely home – a real family home. They lived in a decent part of town, with furniture they chose, not cast-offs from the neighbours. They sat round a proper dining table and ate home-cooked meals together. They weren't left shop-bought Swiss rolls to fend for themselves for tea.

If Barbara, such a caring, level-headed and shrewd lady, thought that we might dare to apply for a mortgage, I thought maybe she was right. Maybe this was the next logical step … but not the only one. Mortgages have a solid, permanent ring about them. Engagements often fizzled out and were broken. A rental agreement could be terminated without much hassle. Setting out on the road to a proper house purchase with a long-term mortgage, that was commitment. Marriage was really what this was all about.

John wasn't going to be able to attend the wedding. John and Rob Smith had decided to make a new life for themselves over in Jersey. On the Wednesday, Pam drove the pair out to East Midlands airport to catch their flight. (I had managed to buy Pam her own mini for £30, which she loved.) John figured with income tax only ten per cent on Jersey, while it was twenty-eight per cent in the UK, he had a better chance of getting ahead out there.

With my brother planning to be over in Jersey, and Mary in Holloway, it meant only my Mam and Nora (no Dad), would make it. It made Mam very proud to see her son married in church, quietly knowing she was soon about to be a grandmother to their child.

Mam had had a serious problem coping with Mary's parenting skills, or lack of them. After I'd seen Bonnie miming Mary's drug use, we knew it was not a safe upbringing for any child. Years before our wedding, Mary had a second child, Paddy. He was just a bag of bones when he was born, due to Mary's drink and drug addiction. Mam had to act. She reported her concerns to the council and the children were put into foster care. They thrived, eventually going to school at St Pat's. Unfortunately, this left Mary free to carry on her reckless lifestyle. I was able to visit the children with Mam, Pam and sometimes Mary. Over time, our own children managed to get to know their cousins too. This is a long-winded way of explaining why Mam was thrilled at the thought of being a grandmother to our impending family.

The other awkwardness that week was that on the day before, Friday, John turned up unexpectedly. He'd been refused entry into Jersey – a big, long-haired, leather-clad bloke staring at signs blankly because he needed glasses: they thought he was on drugs. So, the wild colonial fella was back. I would have my brother at the wedding, but he had no decent clothes. In the wedding photos you can clearly see John squeezed uneasily into a suit I loaned him.

We were trying to keep costs down. Pam had a florist friend who donated the flowers. The family managed to set out a buffet for the reception at St Pat's Club in town. The bar wasn't free. We managed one Rolls Royce to bring the bridesmaids, then to return to fetch Pam. We didn't time the two runs properly, so Pam arrived forty minutes late, but she looked stunning. That February morning was freezing cold, but you'd never guess from the warmth of her smile.

One hundred guests were invited to the Saturday wedding. My oldest friend, Nick Loxley, who was by then living in London, was coming up to be my best man. I was going to have a quiet stag do with old mates, Nige Ridgeway, Dave McIntyre, and Nick. Just the four of us. In hindsight, I might have overdone it a bit in Yates' Wine Lodge. I felt a bit rough on Thursday morning. We had a one-night honeymoon at the Holiday Inn, then it was back to Bardolph Street until we could move into Sylvan Street.

I'd heard about a house for sale on Sylvan Street – I knew the owner. Barbara had loaned us money for the deposit and we secured a mortgage. It was an immaculate house. I bought the house in a pub, signed the paperwork there and all.

We moved in on St Patrick's Day, a month after the wedding. Ryan was born at the General Hospital in June, a hefty seven pounds and fourteen ounces. Pam stayed in a week (the usual time), then was off work for only six weeks. Once work started, Ryan was left with a childminder during the week. Our daughter Kelly was born the following year. Kelly came a few weeks earlier than expected, so only weighed a healthy six and a half pounds, but was just as delightfully perfect as her elder brother.

When Pam and I were living in Sylvan Street, and Pam was pregnant with Kelly, Big Tim came to stay overnight. He couldn't sleep; I got up to check on him and we got talking. He found it hard to explain. He said there were two versions as to why their marriage failed and asked me to try not to believe just the one I'd heard. Kathleen couldn't cope; she'd always be running off to Nora's. The orphanage had taught her nothing, gave her no idea how to manage an ordinary family life. Big Tim reckoned she'd been institutionalised. Men of his generation never thought to pitch in – maybe not to cook, but perhaps bring home some fish and chips; maybe buy some clothes for the kids. Christmas, birthdays, *anything*. Just *be there*. Hold them, tell them bedtime stories, have a kick-about. Maybe it wasn't only Kathleen who had had no experience of a loving parent.

He couldn't stand the nagging, the hassle of it all. He didn't run to Nora, but to the male equivalent: Irish working-class pubs and grim labourers' lodgings.

Knowing Kathleen couldn't cope, he went off to find work further afield, neglecting to send any money back to support his three children or ease the stress on his frazzled wife, who was struggling to make ends meet. When the mines closed, Big Tim joined the army of Irish labourers employed in London's building boom.

Tim and Pam

Tim and Pam on their Wedding Day

Tims Mam Kathleen

Mam and Nora at Tim and Pam's Wedding

Barbara and Denis (Pam's Mam and Dad)

Cousin Tracey, Best Man Nicky Loxley, Tim, Pam, Denis, Pam's Sister Denise, and nieces Andrea and Donna

Chapter Twenty-Nine

Roots and Farewells

Mary's behaviour was a constant stress for us all, especially for Mam. One example was when Mary was due to appear in court on a Drunk and Disorderly charge. Mary was then living with a mixed-race fellow, Paul Williams, a very tough, hard man. He'd been bought up in a Barnardo's Home. Mam contacted him to find out how Mary had got on in court. His curt reply left Mam unsettled.

I heard about this when John and I met up in the Horsefair pub. The way I heard it, our Mam had been disrespected. Paul Williams' regular pub was the Long Stop. I decided to go and sort Williams out, telling John, 'Come along and watch my back.'

Paul was sitting with Mary in a corner by the door. Williams jumped up immediately, knowing there'd be trouble. We started throwing punches at each other. Mary also jumped up and broke a bottle over John's head. Our fight carried on outside. A police car spotted the trouble, pulling up closer to have a look. I heard one officer remark, 'Oh, it's only Williams,' as they drove off.

John's head was bleeding badly. I needed to get him to A&E to get it stitched up, so we headed back to the Horsefair to collect the van's keys. Six cops jumped out of nowhere as we set off. 'Have you been drinking?'

'Yes,' I replied, explaining that my blood-soaked brother urgently needed to get to hospital. They called an ambulance for John.

I lost my licence for eighteen months for drink driving, and I lost my job instantly.

Two days later I saw Paul again and tried to get to the bottom of what he'd said to Mam that had so upset her. He reckoned she'd misunderstood, that she'd got the wrong end of the stick. We ended up both apologising. Paul said he was hurt by my calling him a 'black bastard'. I said I couldn't change what I'd said, it was in the past, but I was sorry and reckoned he was a sound bloke. Paul had tried his best to sort Mary out, but she defeated him too.

He was a good man, Paul Williams. Years later I went to his funeral, determined to pay my respects.

Nora had been in poor health for some time. She'd had cancer, had an operation that left her with a stoma bag, but had been given the all-clear. Five years later she found the cancer had returned. She made it to our wedding, but soon took to her bed. Mam would pop down a couple of times each day to look after her. Like Mack had done years earlier, Nora too moved her bed downstairs. I visited regularly too. We owed her a lot. She didn't have long and was determined to die at home.

Mack and Nora had a special fondness for Mary, their 'Rose of Traleee', so when Mary's life began to unravel, Nora gave her a lot of encouragement, always hoping Mary could one day turn her life around. Nora never gave up on her – her granddaughter as near as could be. I reckon Nora's failure to rescue Mary weighed her down, wore her down. She confided in our priest at St Pat's, the Hungarian

Father Tuto. Maybe he could offer a helping hand to break Mary's self-destructive cycle.

Father Tuto tried his best, but Mary's alcoholism had too tight a stranglehold on her by this point.

In May 1980, I got a phone call to tell me that the priest had been sent for; Nora was dying. With my driving ban still in place I had to find John. He'd be at his usual hang-out, the Standard pub. He was deep asleep across the length of fitted bench seating. We had no time to waste. Rousing him wasn't easy, but we scrambled to get a bus up to Mowmacre Hill.

We were too late. She had just passed when we arrived to say our last farewells. Nora had been paying in weekly to cover her funeral expenses. She was convinced she was covered. When Mam went to sort out Nora's affairs, her accumulated sixpences added up to a pittance. Father Tuto covered the cost. Nora was buried in a communal plot owned by the parish. She was well known. Her funeral, held at an early 9.30 a.m. slot, had a decent, respectful turnout, most of the local Irish community.

As the Mass was ending, Father Tuto came to give a final blessing for Nora, sprinkling the open casket with Holy Water. The heavy church doors were abruptly thrown open, and Mary burst in, telling her waiting taxi to keep his meter running. Obviously blind drunk, she caught sight of Father Tuto standing over Nora. She added insult to injury by swearing at him, 'Get your f*****g hands off my aunt!'

Mam could not stop crying. She disowned her daughter again for shaming our family in front of the whole community. When Nora was laid to rest, the rain had let up and a rainbow arched across the sky. 'She's at peace now,' I said.

When I was still under the driving ban, I worked managing a factory for cash in hand. Getting personally insured as a driver was going to be almost impossible when the ban was due to lift in June 1981. I was fortunate to be taken on by an Indian company, Euro-Light, on Melton Road. They fitted up shops all over the country, including London. They needed me to handle the refrigeration installations. Their vans were covered by fleet insurance, so my personal history was not an issue. I worked with Joe Litt and Adi Patel, and I was taken on just a week before my ban was over.

I was earning decent money then and was entitled to two weeks' holiday in September. I was determined to take Mam to Ireland and see for myself the family farm and the places I had heard so much about over the years. This was partly because my paternal grandmother Mary O'Sullivan had died in 1978, the year Pam and I were married. My grandfather, John, had died years before, so I never had the chance to meet the couple who looked after John those first years of his life. But there were scores of cousins.

Mam had kept in touch with friends and family. She especially missed Sheila O'Connor, who used to be her near neighbour on Mowmacre Hill, and the two girls, Marion and Bridget, who were friends with our Mary. Both girls were now married, and both to men called Liam.

This was the time of the Troubles and Pam was uneasy about going. We would be in an obviously English car, and Pam was obviously not Irish. Posters about the hunger strike were on every lamp post.

But, that September 1981, Pam's dad loaned us his car and we set off for Liverpool to catch the ferry to Dublin, but not before Mam had sprinkled Holy Water all over the car and our heads, as she did every time we went anywhere. We stayed in Clontarf (Dublin) with 'Big' Liam and Marion that first weekend, meeting Bridget and her family there too.

On the Monday we set off to drive to Limerick with Marion to see the farm her dad Billy had inherited, the reason they had to leave Mowmacre Hill. We had a puncture on the way. The roads were full of potholes before money from the EU had built new motorways. We just managed to scrape into the O'Connors' place, Mount Pleasant, Abbey Field. Billy was a force to be reckoned with in that area, and known as a staunch churchgoer, anti-drink, and very keen on the GAA (Gaelic football). We received a *very* warm welcome. Pam and I were not brought up in a rural setting, and the reality of farm life was very soon up close and personal. Billy's wife Sheila (Mam's best friend) had died. The unmarried children, now adults, were busy coping with the milking, mucking out, as well as keeping up with the domestic tasks their late mother would have done.

We found it almost impossible to sleep that first night. Pam was being bitten incessantly by cattle fleas and getting out of bed to layer on as many clothes as she could muster to cover any exposed flesh. At four in the morning she was telling me her unvarnished opinion of Irish rural life, when Mam came through to overhear Pam's fuming. Mam wasn't offended, but was in an equally bad temper. 'If Sheila was alive, she'd have sorted these fleas.' She was sure.

That wasn't all. Mam had been in the next room, sharing with our toddlers, Ryan (three) and Kelly (two). Little Ryan, snuggling next to his granny, had wet the bed. Mam was bitten and drenched. Rest was not an option: she was off to make a pot of tea – the answer to everything.

While the fleas at night were a force to be reckoned with, by day the farm was an adventure playground for Ryan and Kelly. The O'Connors had no telly, but our children loved it there, running wild over the fields, and playing among the haystacks.

Billy sent me off down the road to the local garage to get the flat tyre sorted before we headed off to Cork to explore the O'Sullivan home place. 'Tell them I sent you,' he told me. 'They'll see you right.' When I opened the boot to pack our bags next morning, I saw the useless tyre the fellow had left for our spare. Billy had a 'sharp word' with the garage owner in person and the matter was put right. He apologised, thinking we were only tourists.

The roads being so poor, we stopped halfway to spend a night in a pub that offered B&B. When we finally arrived at the farm inherited by my dad's youngest brother, there was a very old woman sitting out front. We asked for 'Anthony Cumba O'Sullivan'. Cumba is the family name of my branch of the O'Sullivans. In that part of the world, virtually everyone was an O'Sullivan.

The old woman told us he'd gone off years ago. She had no idea where he was, and shooed us away. We were furious. Even strangers would get invited in for a cup of tea in Ireland. We'd come all this way, spent all our savings on a holiday, to be turfed off my own family's home place.

We drove back up the way we'd come to the village. *I need a drink,* was my thought. We needed a place to stay. All the B&Bs had signs saying 'No children'. We were miles from anywhere and hadn't budgeted for this.

The village was run by John Terry O'Sullivan. He ran the pub, the supermarket, the garage, etc. I settled the kids, Pam and Mam with their drinks at a table. I hoped the barman could tell us where we could stay.

John Terry himself it was, and he spotted me for an O'Sullivan by the look of me. I explained about our looking for Anthony Cumba. He laughed. 'That'll be old Nora you met, your grandad's unmarried sister. She'd be fearing you were either the taxman or the Gardai.

Any stranger she'll send away!' He explained the home place was doing very well indeed. The business was split in two: Anthony ran the trawlers, out mackerel fishing, and his wife Eileen ran the farm with its thousands of sheep. Anthony was away out at sea, but he'd phone Eileen and sort it out.

He gave us directions to Veronica's B&B, 'Ocean View'. Her dad was 'Con the Post'. It was a lovely spot, and we stayed there a week. We met our extended family, Anthony, Eileen and their two children, John and Mary. The weather was good and the beach was just down the road. It felt like a proper holiday. We shared a last meal together at Murphy's in Castletown.

Our next stop was to Clonakilty in Skibbereen. By this time, our money was running short. We borrowed £30 from Veronica, which we arranged to repay to her by post. Clonakilty was the orphanage where Mam and Bridget were dumped long ago.

We'd arranged to stay overnight in a pub in Skibbereen, the town where Mam's family is from. Clonakilty is about ten miles away, out of sight of the townsfolk. In 1981 the building was no longer an orphanage, simply a convent. It still looked very imposing, like a big grim workhouse.

Thirty-five years later, Mam stepped up to ring the bell at the heavy wooden door. We were hungry and skint but had no idea how we'd be received. I stood by Mam, to give her confidence. This was a big moment for her.

Two incredibly old nuns opened the door. The older one squinted hard at us both, then broke into a broad smile. 'God bless you, Kathleen O'Callaghan!' I was there as a true witness – that nun recognised her straight away.

We were warmly welcomed, given a proper tea with heaps of sandwiches and a full tour of the place. That old nun must have been a bit confused because she initially thought I was Mam's husband, which had us all laughing. As I was only twenty-four, I must have looked exceedingly worn and stressed, or that dear sister had misplaced her spectacles. The visit was a triumph. Mam was over the moon.

We returned by the fast ferry from Dun Laoghaire, departing at 3.00 a.m., and were back in Leicester by eight. We'd been gone two weeks, and Mam seemed restored, better after that positive revisiting of her past life.

Mary was out on home leave. Pam and I decided to take her out because this was a nice clean start for her. We arranged to take her to Bailey's nightspot in Leicester on Saturday night with our good friends Jan and Vince McKeefery, who actually ended up being our Son and daughters Godparents. Pam bought a lovely gown and she looked gorgeous. We met up in town. We went for a drink in the George and then up to Bailey's. Mary was on half lagers, the same as Pam. The five of us were enjoying the evening. Then Pam picked her half of lager up, and it was full of whiskey. She'd got the wrong drink – she'd picked Mary's up. Mary was filling her drink up from a bottle of whiskey she had stashed. Pam looked at me, nodded, and told me. I thought, *so much for the new start.*

Mary had taken up with Michael, a Mayo man, a nice fellow. They were living in a bed and breakfast in Saxbury Street, across from the Hide pub. One day Mary got knocked down by a bus and was sent to the Royal Infirmary. When I heard this, I told Mam I'd go and visit her in hospital. On Sunday night, I went to visit Mary; Michael was there. Mary seemed alright. I said to her a final time, 'Come on, Mary, let's get a grip of this now.' I gave her a hug and a kiss, and I put my hand in my pocket and whatever money I had I gave to her. I said, 'Get out of this dump, and we'll address things.'

That would be the last I ever saw of Mary. Michael later told us that when she was in the hospital she was so desperate for a drink that she escaped in her pyjamas. She wheeled her drip to the Swan and Rushes pub, next to the hospital.

Mam had a phone call from Michael the following Sunday morning to say Mary had died in her sleep. She was back home by then and he had woken to find her lifeless beside him. That was Sunday 29 November 1981.

Mam rang Pam. She was in bits. I was sent to find John, in the Long Stop as usual, and to contact Dad (Big Tim) over in Grimsby. Even he had had a go at trying to help his daughter. Maybe one reckless, irresponsible drinker could bond with another, or maybe he wanted to test out his latent parenting skills. It didn't work out, and he too felt he'd failed her, and owed it to her to attend her funeral.

It was only a few months since we'd returned from our big holiday in Ireland, reconnecting with our best friends, the O'Connors, who'd once been neighbours on Mowmacre Hill. The two girls who'd known Mary, Bridget and Marion, both came over to support Mam. They stayed a week and were a great support for her.

Father Tuto conducted Mary's funeral too. He had a keen appreciation of what she had endured, the tough hand life had dealt her. 'God's decided she's suffered enough. It's time for her to come home.' Mary was buried in the same communal grave with her aunt Nora. She was only twenty-six.

I was furious to find I'd had a day's wages from my job as a refrigeration engineer docked for attending Mary's funeral. Tensions came to a head at the company Christmas party, when I smacked Adi Patel. I decided it was time to walk out and set up my own business.

Pam managed to get a £500 loan from the TSB. My new life began on 1 February 1982 when I set up TS Refrigeration. It was hard for the first few years with no spare cash for holidays. Pam took on extra work, juggling three jobs while things were tight. But from the day I became my own boss, there was no looking back.

Tim's 60th outside The Addies with all the family

Johnny, Paddy, Tim, Lee and Ryan

John, Mam and Tim at the Tudor Rose, Mowmacre Hill.
Mary's first anniversary.

Chapter Thirty

Fresh Arrivals, Sad Departures

After a few years things were going great for TS Refrigeration and John worked for me when we needed him. Kevin took over all the engineering side and I dealt with installs and cold rooms, big plants and rip-outs, John working for me.

John and I were in the Longstop one Friday night and John had put his hand in his pocket to buy us a pint. A guy tapped him on the shoulder and said, 'Excuse me a wee minute, you've dropped this,' and handed him a five-pound note that he had dropped. Five pounds was a lot of money in those days. They got chatting; the guy's name was Thomas McMullen, but I later called him 'Bogside Tom'. He was from White Rock, Falls Road, Belfast. His story was that his sister had got friendly with a British soldier and the IRA petrol-bombed the house because she wouldn't end her relationship. The house burned down, so he had to move in with another sister in Belfast. He was a gravedigger by profession but he worked at British Shoe, a massive depot up in Braunston. He had been a petty criminal in Belfast. He was told by the IRA after a couple of warnings to move out. When he didn't they kidnapped him – put a hood on him, threw him in the back of a van and took him to a warehouse where they threatened to kneecap him. Classic. They told him to leave Belfast and never return, so he was run out of town. By that time, the British soldier, who was from Leicester, had left the army. He sent for Bogside's sister. She came over and they set up home in Leicester. When Bogside was run out of Belfast, he moved in with her. He got the nickname 'Bogside' from me. He was also known as Belfast Tommy, but I knew a Belfast Jimmy. I thought it had more of a ring to it, Bogside Tom. He became a half brother to John and me over the years. Whatever we did, he was always there. He moved in with John, and it was like Laurel and Hardy. Bogside used to come into work.

In 1978, when Margaret Thatcher came into power, John had said, 'I'm not working for that Tory bitch. In fact, I'm not going to work this century', and he actually managed to pull that off by 1998. John did plenty of work for cash, but what I class as work is getting a wage packet and paying tax, cash in hand does not qualify as work to me. And then you only work two days a week and have Mondays and Fridays off. That's how things were. When John got a flat up at Iona Close, we called it Iona Mansions, Bogside moved in, and they shared a flat.

Bogside got the sack from the British Shoe for spitting on the work bus; he was not allowed on it, and then they booted him out. Bogside had lived a sheltered life in Belfast apart from his petty criminalism. He never mentioned girlfriends. John said that Bogside was a twenty-three-year-old virgin and thought fucking a bird was stealing her purse. He eventually met a strange woman who bore him a couple of kids, and then we never saw much of him. The Jehovah's Witnesses knocked on his door one day and said, 'You mean to say you're not married?' So they got married, and John was the best man. What a laugh that was, in Pocklington's Walk. None of the women in Bogside's family would come over because they looked upon a woman with kids as a trollop. They would have nothing to do with her. But his brothers came over with his dad, and what a lovely fellow he was.

I made sure John looked smart for the wedding. As the registrar was reading the marriage vows out, towards the end, we heard Bogside's dad say loudly, 'I can't hear a fucking word that woman is saying.' Of course, we all burst out laughing. The registrar was fuming, but she finished the marriage ceremony. Outside, I said to the brothers, 'What was all that about? The outburst?'

They said, 'The silly fucker. He was peeing in the bucket last night and his hearing aid fell into the bucket of piss and it fucked it up.' So he couldn't hear a thing.

And that was Bogside married. Then Bogside faded for a bit. We didn't see much of him.

My dad used to ring me but not very often as he couldn't work a phone; someone else would always make the call and then they would hand him the phone. Later in life he lived in Grimsby, his own flat over a bookmaker's, with a lady called Georgina, who had two sons from a previous marriage. He'd been with her on and off for twenty years. He was working in the building trade. John and I went to see him. John thought Grimsby was going to be another London, but it was a shit hole. We came away early on the Sunday. A few months down the line, we got a call from Georgina, who I had got to know well; she was a decent, lovely woman. She rang me to say Dad had had an accident. He'd slipped going up the metal staircase to his flat in the rain. He'd banged his head and was in the hospital.

I phoned the hospital because I was the next of kin. The consultant said, 'Come over, and I'll chat to you face to face.' So John and I went over to Grimsby to see Dad in hospital. He seemed alright. I then saw the surgeon, who explained that when they did the scans on my dad, they found a brain tumour that had been dormant all his life – it must have developed when he was a teenager. This was the first time he'd ever been sick in his life, and it activated the tumour. I told the surgeon that when Dad was sixteen, he took a beating in Tottenham by six fellas. He said that was obviously the cause of the tumour. It had lain dormant all his life, but it was active now, and it wasn't looking very good for him.

They discharged him, but he was in a wheelchair, and he needed twenty-four-hour all-around care. Georgina, fair play to her, moved back in. They brought the bed downstairs, and that was that. It was a case of wait and see. He lasted another eighteen months. I remember getting a call on the landline at home that he had been taken seriously ill. The hospital rang up Friday night, but I'd been out drinking. They told Pam I should go to Grimsby because it was not looking good. She woke me, and I said, 'I can't go to Grimsby, it's a four or five-hour drive, and I've been out drinking. It's the middle of the night. I'll go in the morning.'

But the phone rang at seven o'clock on Saturday morning. It was the hospital, and they said he'd passed away; it was 7 December 1985. They said I'd have to come over and collect the death certificate. I asked if Georgina could collect it, but they said it had to be the next of kin. I went over, saw Georgina, and did the necessary. I decided that we would bring Dad home to Leicester and bury him with Mary and Nora because, in years to come, nobody would ever have visited a grave in Grimsby.

Tim and Ryan, outside the GPO, O'Connel Street, Dublin, 1981

Mam and Tim at Grandad's headstone
(Grandad died in Aillihies in 1979 aged 84)

Anthony and Eileen's children. John and Mary. Tim's cousins

Billy O'Connor and some of his kids

On holiday in Aillihies, Southern Ireland.
Dave, Kelly, Nealle, Uncle Anthony, Kathy and Pam.

Tim, Mam and Anthony.
Aillihies, West Cork.

Gumba O'Sullivan's Farm - Anthony's

Tim in later years

Chapter Thirty-One

New Horizons

I was better off financially now. I'd been in business for three years, and money was rolling in. When we went to the undertakers they wanted £280 to get him back to Leicester and I explained that he actually lived in Grimsby when he died, and that was a lot of money, so I said I would be in touch. I found another undertaker and I told him my dad had been visiting Grimsby, and because he wasn't living there he was happy to go and fetch him for only an extra £30. Apparently, there's an old law where undertakers have to pay each county for the privilege of driving through it with a body. But anyway, we got him back, and his Mass was at St Patrick's church. I had bought the grave back from St Patrick's parish. A lady called Audrey Jelly, who had lived a similar life to Mary, was buried in the plot. I said, 'Don't worry. I will honour that lady and put her name on the headstone.' Years later I was having a conversation in the pub and a guy I knew called Drew said, 'I wish I knew where my mother was buried.' After a bit more chatting he said her name was Audrey Jelly. We talked about her age when she died and we realised she was the lady in our plot. That grave became our family plot.

My dad's brother, Uncle Anthony, came over from Ireland with Eileen. A minibus full of Irish fellas also came from Grimsby. I met them at St Patrick's Church and they came to the cemetery. I directed them to the wake, it was out of the cemetery, to turn right and take the next right to the Addies Bar. We never saw them again. They ended up somewhere in town in an Irish bar. But we had a good drink on the Old Fella.

A couple of years later I got Ryan his first computer, an Amstrad, and one game. Kevin, bless him, sorted it all out. I said, 'I want it to be all working when Christmas Day comes.' Kevin was my engineer from TS. I remembered some of the nightmares I'd had on Christmas Day, putting bikes together. So, it was all set. The kids woke up at 4 a.m., excited as anything, and got me up. I let them see the computer surprise and they were over the moon. Ryan was excited and switched it on, but we couldn't get it to work. Fair play to Kevin, I rang him at half past four on Christmas Day, and he came over and sorted it all out for Ryan. Ryan got on with it. At about half seven, we got the kids ready for Christmas Mass. I had planned we'd go to Mass, drop Mam off at home, pick John up, go back for Mam, then go for a drink.

I decided I'd get John. He could come to Mass – he hadn't been for years. So I loaded up the kids in the van and headed for Iona Mansions. I beeped the horn and John looked out of the window, signalled me, and down he came. 'Merry Christmas,' he said to the kids. He said, 'Have you got my score?' I told him I'd give it to him later. He was referring to his twenty pounds. I would buy all the drinks, and he would get twenty pounds, which would sort him out for Christmas night and Boxing Day.

We headed for St Pat's; I could see Mam chatting with three or four of her Irish biddies as I drove up. One of the ladies spotted the van. 'Here's Timmy,' Mam said, 'he's got the children with him.'

John said to me, 'What the fuck are we doing here?'

I said, 'You're going to go to Mass.'

He said, 'I ain't going.'

I said, 'You are. Get out. Otherwise, you ain't getting your twenty pounds.'

He slid the door open, and Mam said, 'Jesus Christ, Timmy, what have you brought that scruff with you for?'

And without a second thought, John shouts back, in front of all of her friends, 'Merry Christmas, Mam, are you still in arrears with your rent?' Mam was fuming.

Anyway, we got into the church, Mam on the front row, as usual, not to be missed by the priest. Me, John, Ryan and Kelly sat next to her on the same pew. And all John was barking about was, 'Where's my twenty pounds?'

I said, 'I'll sort you out your money. Enjoy the Christmas Mass.' Oh, he was fuming. The plate came around. I had a ball of money. I took a twenty-pound note and a pound note out of my pocket. I said to John as the plate came, 'Here's your money.' I dropped the twenty-pound note into the plate. I had deliberately dropped the twenty in and pretended it was a mistake. I said, 'Oh, sorry, John, I've dropped it in the plate by accident.'

John said, 'Hang on, hang on, bring that back. There's been a mistake. Excuse me! Bring it back.' He started moving down the aisle for the plate. Mam hadn't seen the twenty-pound note going in. She thought he was trying to rob the plate in front of everybody. Oh, it was a laugh. When we got outside, Mam was raging. John shouted, 'Where is my twenty pounds?'

I said, 'It's on the plate.' I let it run for a bit and then I gave him the money.

I took the kids home. Mam and John came in to say Merry Christmas to Pam. We went up to the Tudor Rose and had a Christmas drink. John came back to our house. And that was Christmas over.

When Ryan and Kelly were school age we wanted to send them both to St Pat's. The headmaster was Mr Woods and he organised for both of them to start there. It was very emotional visiting the same school again. I went into the tiny little toilets – it brought all the memories back. Nothing had changed at St Pat's since the days – the two separate playgrounds, the same classrooms. The first day of school was a proud day. We took them down there and walked them in. There were no big scenes. No haemorrhages. No ambulances. Unlike John's and my first day there. They settled in.

By this time TS was flying with a lot of long hours and hard work. And I had a lock-up under the Tigers' ground that could accommodate a forty-foot container full of refrigeration. I was the Leicester agent for the Elcold brand of refrigeration equipment. They were based in Denmark and it meant trips to visit facilities in Denmark, France and Germany, which I eagerly took. Things were going well.

The kids were growing up so I wanted to plan our first holiday outside Ireland. There was a little travel agent down the road. They suggested Ten Bel in the Canaries, Tenerife. They didn't have any brochures, but they assured me it was a hotel where the kids could have adjoining rooms and everything was great. Well, that turned out to be the first holiday disaster. We landed in Tenerife and got on the bus. Some lady got up and announced herself as Auntie Jean. She was telling us what was at the hotel. She said that the breakfast every morning would be hung on our door during the night. I said, 'Excuse me, Auntie Jean, we're on the wrong bus. We're going to a four-star hotel.'

She said that was correct. I said, 'What's this breakfast hanging on the door about? How can you hang egg and bacon on the door?'

She said, 'No, it's a continental breakfast.' I said again that we were on the wrong bus. She checked the form and said, 'No, you're on the right bus.'

We arrived at Ten Bel. What a dump. It was an old Pontin's camp – more like an old prisoner-of-war camp. I went into the office and spoke to the manager, a young cockney about my age. I said, 'There's been a mistake. We've been booked into the wrong place. I booked a four-star hotel.'

He said, 'This is a four-star hotel.'

I said, 'No, it's not. It fucking ain't. A hotel starts at the ground and goes up into the sky.' I demonstrated with my hands.

He said, 'This is a hotel complex.'

I leaned over the side of the counter, grabbed him by the scruff of the neck and dragged him over to my side. The female reps came over and broke it up. I said, 'I want a hotel. A proper hotel, not this fucking dump.'

Meanwhile, the kids had decided to strip off and jump in the swimming pool in their underpants and knickers, to the shock of some guests. Anyway, the manager assured me that he would take us around tomorrow and see if he could get us into a hotel. In the meantime, he sent a rep to show us where we would be staying.

When we picked up the bags and got to the room, I said, 'Where's the kids' room?'

He said, 'Oh, it's down there, 150 metres away.'

I said, 'Are you thick?'

We decided to unpack a minimum and deal with it the next day. When Pam unpacked, we realised somebody had stolen her purse. It just went from worse to worse. The manager took me around the hotels, and they were all full up. I got back, and I decided, sorry, we were just going to have to stop there, make the most of it, and then sue the bastards when we got back. That night, Ryan and Kelly slept with us in the bed. Then they moved us to a family room the next day. I rang up the person who was looking after TS and said, 'Get on to that travel agent because we're going to nail them.' We moved into the family room, and we decided we wanted breakfast. A proper breakfast, none of that continental shite. We went to the supermarket, did a load of shopping, filled up the fridge and got on with it.

We went around the pool, and I said to the kids, 'Don't laugh and smile!' Video cameras were all the thing at that time. The reps were all out with video cameras. I said, 'Don't let them see you smile. You're miserable because you're in this shite hole.' We went for something to eat, went back to the hotel and went to bed.

Next morning, Pam was ready to cook us a nice breakfast. And guess what, the fucking fridge was broken. Everything was thawed out and gone off. It couldn't get any worse. Anyway, we were about three or four days into it, starting to make friends. We got on with it. We thought we would hire a car and go up to Mount Teide to break the monotony of playing games around the pool. We hired a little red Fiat, and off we went into the mountains. Coming back, the car broke down. I managed to pull into the village and phone the necessary people. We were there for three hours, baked alive on the side of the mountain. So what else could go wrong?

The second week flew by. We'd made decent friends there and enjoyed it. When we got back, I said to the travel agents, 'I am taking you to court.' There were no brochures; they were at fault. They should have explained. Anyway, they gave me £1,200 back out of the £1,600 I paid. So that wasn't too bad.

We plodded on. A couple of years went by and Disney and Florida was the big thing then, but it was expensive. But we decided to make up for that Ten Bel nightmare and go to Disney. So we set off. A week in Miami and a week in the Bahamas. We landed in Miami. We were staying in a proper hotel! On the beach – Collins Avenue. We enjoyed being in America. We decided we would go to Disney. We would get the bus up there; it was only two hours. We spent the night there and had a great time. It lived up to everything we had heard about it. Then back to Miami for a couple of days. I bought the kids a blowup alligator.

We were on the beach and the kids were playing in the sand. I went into the water but I heard Pam and the kids screaming.

I looked up and saw the ''gator', as the yanks call them, was blowing down the beach. I set off chasing it. In the meantime, two lifesavers had spotted it. They both looked like David Hasselhoff from *Baywatch*. I managed to get to the gator first, and they shouted, 'Hey, buddy, put that down. It belongs to that lady and those children.'

I said, 'Yeah, I know that. I'm their dad.'

They said, 'Put it down.'

I said, 'Will I fuck.'

Anyway, they shouted over to Pam, 'Hey, ma'am, do you know this guy?' And she said she'd never seen me before in her life.' They told me to drop the gator, otherwise, they would drop me. So I dropped it, and they picked it up and took it over to Pam and the kids. What a twat I felt.

All that night Pam and the kids were saying, 'You got sand kicked in your face.' Pam was to blame. It was hysterical when we looked back.

A couple of days later, we flew to the Bahamas and had a good time there. We were in a two-star hotel with all the yank workers. They were on their holidays. They were as good as gold. Money was running short by then. I was on the back end of £2,000; in those days it was a lot of money, so we decided we would eat in the room. Cheese sandwiches for the last couple of days, and my Budweiser bought from the shop. And at night, we would sit in the bar and I would order one Budweiser. Then Ryan would be up and down in the lift to get me the cold ones out of the fridge. The lady would say, 'My Gawd, I've never seen someone get so happy on one tin of Budweiser.' Little did she know, I was on my eighth of the night.

Another day in the Bahamas, we came out of the pool and sat on the patio. I said to Ryan, 'Put your feet up.' He put his feet on the chairs in front. I said, 'Remember this day. You're in paradise.'

All of a sudden, we heard, 'Hey, buddy, get out of the sun. You're burning up.'

I said to Ryan, 'Do you hear what that prat is shouting at somebody?' Ryan giggled.

And the next thing I knew, 'Hey buddy,' the guy tapped me on the shoulder, 'get out of the sun, you're burning up!'

I said, 'Fucking burning up? It's my Irish blood. I'm always this colour. Fuck off.' He was a big fella. Texan. He went into the toilet. Pam had arrived with Kelly then, and Ryan told them what had happened.

'Oh, here we go again, sand kicked in your face.'

I said, 'We'll see what sand is when he comes out of the toilet.' I swear he never came out, and when I went in to look, the window was open. But that was the sort of fun we had.

At night, there was a lovely bar, the Green Shutters, that I would visit. Pam got invited to the governor's house with other guests from the hotel. It was a form of welcome, thanking people for using the Bahamas.

Anyway, there was a good view of the marina from the bar. The yachts and speedboats pulled up because there was no gambling in Florida, so they would all come to the Bahamas. It had some massive casinos.

I was chatting to an American guy there one night. By this time we were low on our funds. He said, 'Do you want a bucket of chicken?' Ryan and I thought that would be nice, and he bought us one each. We scoffed it all. It was beautiful chicken wings and legs. The next night, we were in there again. The same guy came in, nice fellow. We got chatting and drinking. He said, 'Are we having chicken tonight? A bucket of chicken tonight?'

I said, 'No, we're not bothering.' I didn't have the money.

He said, 'That's a shame. Well, I'll get mine.' He got himself a bucket; he was eating it and we were staring at him. He said, 'Are you sure you guys don't want something to eat?' So we helped ourselves. In the end, he said to us, 'Here, have the lot. I thought you weren't hungry.' Anyway, that ended that friendship. But we managed to scrape through. And it was one of the best holidays we would have. We returned to Florida a few years later and rented a five-bedroom villa. We had a great time, again.

Kelly, Pam, Ryan and Tim

Bonnie, Mary and Paddy

Chapter Thirty-Two

The Next Generation

Ryan and Kelly were developing their own characters by now. Ryan was taking after me. He watched me when I had the Teletext on all afternoon when we weren't working – checking the share prices. I was buying currencies. I bought a load of Irish Punts because I would be in Ireland regularly anyway. But it was at such a low price. I bought a few thousand pounds' worth. When Ireland joined the Euro-Zone, that was all converted into Euros, which produced a hefty profit. Every nationalised company – BT, British Gas, East Midlands Electric – every one, I bought what they would allow me, a couple of thousand each. So I had a good portfolio of shares and unit trusts.

The Bank of Ireland brought one out and we all jumped on that. It was doing well. Ryan used to watch me studying share prices. His birthday was coming up. I remember saying to him, 'Right, Ryan, I am going to give you a hundred pounds for your birthday. I know you're after some Nike trainers, but why don't you invest a hundred pounds in the stock market. Pick a share of your choice. You know, you've been watching and studying for a bit. Then in five years, have another look at those shares, and you'll see a difference.'

Ryan had a shrewd mind; he said, 'I'll buy trainers for £50 and £50 worth of shares.'

I thought, *Cute little man.*

Kelly was into animals early on. They hounded me to get a pet and we settled for a baby rabbit. Kelly would dress it in doll's clothing and put it in a doll's pram, then push it around the street. She turned it into a baby. But the dogs would hound her, they would smell the rabbit. I had to keep an eye on her. That's the way Kelly was. She was developing into a lovely little girl. She thought the world was made of candyfloss. And that was how I wanted to keep it for her. Ryan got his first job while he was still at school. He got a paper round at Molsbury's newspaper shop, and the funny thing was it was my exact paper round from when I was a kid and worked for the same shop. It was an early morning round and one morning, when it was throwing it down with rain, he woke me up to take him round. So I ended up driving around in a Mercedes to deliver newspapers.

I was visiting Mam one Saturday, and she mentioned that Paddy had been caught sniffing glue up in Coalville. I waited until the next weekend to picked him up on it. I dropped Mam and Bonnie at Mam's and took Paddy up to the cemetery. When we got there, I dragged him out of the Merc, threw him on the grave and said, 'Listen, there's one spot left there. Start digging. If you're carrying on with the glue, it won't stop there. It will be something else, and something else. And before you know where you are, you'll be at your mother's level, shooting needles.' He burst out crying and started to claw away at the earth. Anyway, I picked him up and put him back in the car.

By the time, Bonnie had turned eighteen. She left the foster home and got a flat. As soon as she was settled in, we helped with furniture and money. She applied to become Paddy's guardian. He basically had a large cupboard for his bedroom. It worked out great. Bonnie and Paddy were so happy. We would pick them up every two or three weeks and take them out around Coalville, then bring them back to Leicester.

On one visit I noticed a big picture of Bob Marley on Paddy's wall. And he was talking like a black fella, which was quite funny and we'd joke with him about it. Later I said to Mam, 'You know that Michael Jackson? How he's taking pills to turn himself white?'

She said, 'Yes, I read about it.'

I said, 'Paddy's taking pills to turn himself into Bob Marley.'

She said, 'Oh, God almighty, what are we going to do with him? I can't explain to people that a ginger-haired, freckled face young boy will be turning into a black man.'

I howled with laughter. You could tell Mam anything in a convincing voice and she would believe it. And that is how it went on with Bonnie and Paddy.

Later I discovered that Lee was living with his mam in Thurmaston. She had got married again to a guy called Peg. Lee was working for a fruit and veg bloke in Thurmaston, who just happened to be one of the customers that we did work for in his fridges and cold rooms. I knew him quite well.

One day I decided to ring up and speak to Lee. When he came on the phone, I just said, 'I'm your father, Tim O'Sullivan. I'd like to meet you and have a chat.' Lee was sixteen then. He'd left school early because he had a job, and he was working for this guy. We met, and everything went from there.

At Christmas, 1989, I was watching the TV, and there was a programme about the St Patrick's Day parade in New York. I thought,

It's one of my dreams to go there. They showed St Patrick's Day march, everything. I decided there and then. Dave McIntyre watched the last ten or fifteen minutes, and I said to him, 'I'm going to go there next year.' I thought it would be a good idea to take Lee. So I asked him and he jumped at the idea. I said we'd have to get him a passport. He was only nineteen at the time. I explained to him that you had to be twenty-one to drink in America, but I had heard we could blag it. Chrissy Conlon, a good friend I used to see regularly in town, had a brother who had a bar in New York, the Blarney Castle, and he told me the address. I said, 'I'll have my lad with me.' He told me not to worry about that, the lads would be alright in the Irish bars, and there were thousands of them.

So that was that; we decided to get him a passport, and while we were at it, to change his name to his original birth name. His name was Lee Timothy O'Sullivan on his birth certificate. Then it was changed to Lee Barnacle; Timothy was dropped. Then it was switched to Lee Edward Davison. We changed it back to Lee Edward O'Sullivan. Eddie, his grandad, had taken ill the year before and passed on, so as a mark of respect, he kept the Edward.

Lee said, 'Can I bring a good friend with me? Daz Kent?' Well, yes, I thought, he was a young buck. *He won't want to be dragging around with me throughout the holiday.* So we were all set for New York.

I met Daz the day we went. Nice, great lad, cheerful, big fellow. We set off and the excitement was oozing out of us all.

We landed at Kennedy Airport at about five o'clock in the afternoon. We went through customs, no problem – we were there for St Pat's Day. Most of the immigration officials had Irish names. There were a lot of Irish there; it put a smile on their faces. They said, 'You've come all this way, for St Patrick's Day?' I told them it was a dream come true.

On the way out of Kennedy Airport, a guy asked us if we wanted a limo into Manhattan. I thought that would be a nice thing. He was only a small guy. We followed him and got into this limo. It was not a stretch limo, but it was a flash car. I sat in the front and the two boys in the back. I looked at the driver; his clothes were a bit shabby. I thought, how can you dress like that, and drive a car like this? We got stuck in the traffic, which was normal on Brooklyn Bridge. I suggested the lads get out and have a look at the sights. We were on Brooklyn Bridge without moving for around twenty minutes. It was a lovely sight to look into Manhattan and back into Brooklyn.

Then we got back in and the traffic was moving, but it was slow. The driver was on the phone constantly, speaking in Italian. I was thinking, *Fuck me, have I made a mistake here?* He'd picked us up from the airport, knowing we were going to have balls of money on us. We were tourists. He knew we wouldn't have weapons – who the hell was he? And where was he taking us? But true to his word, he pulled up outside O'Hallaran House Hotel in Midtown Manhattan. I was glad to get there; it was a good result. He said, 'If ever you need me, here's my card. Call any time.' I thought, well, we got out of that one, but I'd be wary. New York, at the time, was lawless. The murder rate was through the roof. The police were threatening strike action. Nobody cared. If the police went to an incident – and I witnessed a few – they wouldn't get out of the car. They'd just point the gun out of the car and tell the perpetrators to get down on the ground, and they'd wait until it was safe before they would get out.

I was happy to walk into O'Hallaran's Hotel. The first night, I made some enquiries. We showered and wanted to go to the Blarney Castle, but I forgot the address. I was told there were five or six Blarney Castles. I thought, *Fucking hell, what are we going to do now?* We had a drink in the hotel, then we thought we would go for a walk. We found ourselves on Lexington Avenue, Midtown Manhattan when we went out. Across the road, facing the armoury, was O'Reilly's bar. I said, 'We'll go in here.' It was a pure Irish bar with ginger-haired bar staff. They welcomed us and we got chatting. The boss, O'Reilly, came over. He was from the same place Barry McGuigan came from – he knew Barry McGuigan and his dad. I said, 'I was at the fight when he won the title, in London.' We clicked. He asked how long we were there for, and I said five days.

He said, 'Anything you want, just let me know. I'll come and pick you up tomorrow and take you for lunch' So, we were made. I asked him about this Blarney Castle. He said, 'Leave it with me.' I told him the guy's name was Michael Conlon, that he'd been in America for fifty years; he served in the US Army. He said, 'I'll find out which one.' He came back and gave me the address. One, First Street. It was too late now to go – we were knackered by then. I decided we would have a look at that tomorrow.

We went back to the hotel and had a good sleep, three of us were in the same room with a double bed and a camp bed. I thought I would let the boys have the double bed. The camp bed would do for me. I was up early in the morning and I suggested we go and have a wander around. We came out and found Lexington Avenue. We walked and walked. It must have been five miles. We passed sights like Trump Tower, the Rockefeller Centre, St Pat's Cathedral. I couldn't wait to get there.

Eventually, after an hour and a half, I found the Blarney Castle on First Street, with the lads. It had the longest bar I had seen. It was massive. Only a small front but big inside. They told me Micheal Conlon would be in at dinner time, later on. Which he was, and we had a chat with him and his brother. He said, 'Anything you want, we're here.' We had a drink and headed back up Fifth Avenue this time. We saw all the sights there, the shops.

And back to the hotel. The lads were getting a bit fed up with the Irish bars. They had nothing in common with them. So, the main craic was Greenwich Village. So I said, 'Let me go out tonight. We'll get a cab and drop you down Greenwich Village. You know where the hotel is. You've got your key.' And that's what I did. And when I got home around two in the morning, they were in bed watching TV and eating pizzas. I asked if they'd had a good night. They didn't say much. I think the long end of it was that they were down in Greenwich Village, and they were terrified and decided to come back to the hotel. Anyway, I went to the parade on St Pat's Day and they came out that night and we went for a drink. And then I ended up in O'Reillys and went down to the Blarney Castle.

On Sunday, I realised we'd hardly seen anything, so I would find out where we could hire a helicopter, and do the trip.

We got in the helicopter, and it was brilliant. Three German tourists were facing us, young lads, and us three. The trip was in and out of the Twin Towers. We flew around the Statue of Liberty and over the Empire State Building. We didn't miss much. But the smell was horrendous. It stank in there. I could see the Germans looking at us. I looked at the two lads and their socks and trainers. I knew what it was. I said to them, 'You fucking stink.'

They said, 'What you on about? It ain't us.'

It took the edge off the trip. The Germans couldn't wait to get out and breathe fresh air when we landed. We got out, and I said to the lads, 'That fucking stinks. You ruined that trip.' They said it wasn't them, it was the helicopter. I said, 'Well, he must be parking it in our hotel at night because the same fucking smell's in there.' Anyway, I forgave them. I said, 'Right, you want to get some Timberland boots then? Right, I want to go up to the Bronx, and we'll have a look at Fordham Road.'

We tried to get a cab to the Bronx but the drivers wouldn't go near it. Eventually, it cost $22 to go – a Polish taxi driver took us. We had to get out on a dual carriageway and walk down a grass embankment to get to Fordham Road. He wouldn't go actually into the Bronx. We went for a look around and found a big sports shop. There were two big black fellows at the door of the sports shop with baseball bats. I presumed they were security. They searched us and patted us down.

I told the lads I'd wait for them while they tried on the Timberland boots. While I was there, some black guy went out, smartly dressed, wearing a mac, not carrying anything. He set off the alarm on the door. Those two boys on the door didn't mess. They stopped him with a bat. Inside his coat, he had some jeans. The next thing you know, they'd whacked him with their bats, levelled him, put a tie wrap on him, and phoned the police. I hoped the lads didn't get any ideas of having it away with those Timberlands.

They bought their boots at a good price. You could buy them in the Bronx, New York, for half the price of back home. We took the subway back to Manhattan for one dollar. The whole place was full of graffiti; it looked like the film *Warriors*.

Anyway, it was our last night. We said goodbye to all the lads in O'Reilly's and the Blarney Castle. I came back to the room and the lads were eating pizzas again and watching porn films.

In the morning, we checked out. I was asked if I'd had anything out of the minibar. I said, 'I've had a Britvic orange. One orange.' They checked the computer, and it just oozed out paper with goods printed on it. It reached the floor. And I said, 'Hang on, I've had one Britvic orange.'

The desk clerk said, 'Well, someone has had pizzas delivered and bought films.'

So I said, 'How much is a Britvic orange? Well, there is the $2. The rest of it is down to this pair.' And they had to pull up. I was howling with laughter.

We headed to the airport. They weren't in much of a mood. When we landed, Daz Kent thanked me very much and shook my hand.

Lee got fed up working where he was, so I got him a job working with Lee O'Brien as a plastering trainee. He became a good, fast plasterer. He got his best friend at the time, Toby, plastering too. The two of them set their own business up and they did very well. Lee became closer to us over time, we ended up taking him to Ireland with the family one summer as well, we all had a great time. He loved the fishing. One session out on the rocks down by the farm, we caught ninety-six mackerel. We went around the village, giving out the mackerel. It had to be used, it was fresh. Lee loved it.

When John's son Jonny was around eight or nine, Ann decided to let John see him. John would have him every fortnight or so. Poor Jonny spent most of his time in the Friar Tuck or the Robin Hood with a bag of crisps and a bottle of pop, while John got drunk. After a while of that, he'd say, 'I want to go up to Tim and Pam's house.' So he would find his way up to our place. We would make a fuss of him and look after him. He loved it in our home. He'd play with Ryan and Kelly in the garden. And that's how things went on for a few years. We watched Jonny grow up and it was a pleasure. He opened up more and more. Before we knew it, Jonny was looking for work. He had a couple of mediocre jobs when he left school. We got him into the plastering like Lee and he never looked back. He got a job on the council with Harry Witmore, who was a friend of ours. He was his foreman. Jonny was doing well. He went to football matches. He made friends. He ended up with the nickname *Boom Boom*. I said, 'What's all that about?'

Somebody said, 'If someone upsets Jonny, the next thing you hear is *boom boom*, and they're on the floor.'

So he could fight as well.

It was a pleasure to watch him mature into a young man. Eventually, he met a great girl, Michelle. She had a child, Danny, from a previous relationship. Her partner had been knocked down and killed in a motorbike accident. He was only about nineteen. So young Jonny brought Danny up as his own, and went on to have three daughters. Each time we prayed for a boy – we wanted a boy to carry on the O'Sullivan name.

I'd see Jonny regularly with Michelle if we were in town. We'd arrange to meet or we would invite them over to our house. It was lovely watching John's grandchildren grow up into three lovely girls.

Chapter Thirty-Three

Homeland

I'd heard a couple of properties were up for sale in Allihies. I decided to go back and have a look. John had been off the drink for about five months, so I said, 'How would you like to go back for a week? I'll pay for everything. You just bring your beer money.' He'd need a fortune. Ryan jumped at the chance to come. I spoke to a very good friend of mine, Tom Cassie, who I'd drink with every night in the Addies. He was a very good roofer; he had his own business with men working for him. I wanted his advice as I'd heard that one of the roofs was a bit rough.

So we decided that we would go. John was telling everyone it was his first holiday, at forty years old. I'd seen half the world by then, while I could still take a good punch I have been to two world cups and followed Ireland when Jack Charlton was manager. We went to Italy 1990, and USA 1994. Ireland were never going to win the World Cup but we had a good drink trying. We were getting the plane to Cork from Birmingham airport, and when we arrived at the airport we went for breakfast. John saw Tom and me eating breakfast and said, 'How much is that?' I told him it was £10. He said, 'Fuck that,' and got himself a sausage sandwich, which he tore into. I thought he had eaten his fingers, he was that hungry. I told him to go to duty-free and get fags because I didn't want him begging me all holiday.

So we went off with Ryan. Ryan had to make sure he was okay as he had never been to an airport. He had his first pint in six months. I wondered then, was I ready for this?

The flight to Cork was only an hour. We hired a car when we arrived and they gave us a brand-new one with only about forty miles on the clock, a Ford Escort. We had a three-hour drive over the Cork mountains; we stopped halfway in Bantry Bay, had a couple of pints and something to eat, and then headed into Allihies. We were stopping at John Terry's place.

So John was back in his homeland. I went out that night with him and he didn't hold back. He made up for six months off the drink. Pints of Guinness were flying down him. He soon settled in, in the village.

We went down for breakfast in the morning, and John asked Mary-Kelly Terry what time the shop opened. She was married to young John Terry who was the same age as me. They were the owners of the B&B and the shop next door.

'Nine o'clock, John. What are you after?'

He said, 'I want a bottle of Martini.'

I said, 'Fuck me, John. It isn't even nine o'clock.'

She said, 'You'll have to wait until nine o'clock, but if you were desperate for something, I would get it for you.'

After breakfast, we headed up to Danny Dinnish's. Danny had returned to Allihies after fifty years of building the Underground in London. His uncle had come back from America and built a beautiful house on the shore where Danny lived. His wife stayed in Coventry with their three daughters. We took him a box of groceries because he was getting on a bit. He remembered John as a kid. He used to court Auntie Teresa in London, my dad's sister, so we had a lot in common. We would meet him every time we were on holiday in Ireland.

We headed into Castletownbere for something to eat at Murphy's – beautiful home-made food. And then we went on the drink in Castletown. There wasn't much happening in Allihies in the daytime. It was October, so the weather was pretty bleak. John just hit the drink, full bore.

Tom and I went out to see the properties. One of them was a pure shack and I wasn't impressed. The price was OK, but it was too far away for me to keep an eye on the building. A couple of years earlier, I was going to buy a place on the beach, a beautiful stone house for 27,000 punts. I brought the boys in from Bantry to assess it. The architect found damp in the footings. He said it was going to cost another 15,000 punts, which would make it a 40,000-punt house, and it wasn't worth it. What a fool I was. So I pulled out. I had just bought Mam's house in Mowmacre Hill. I wanted to be careful. I didn't want to go into debt and live a life like Mam. So we shelved that. But I thought the house wouldn't be so much. But damp in the footings, you're talking about a major operation. JCBs and everything. They were too far out. You'd have to drink and drive. You couldn't walk down to the village, especially at night. So we decided not to go ahead, and we just got on with the holiday.

I got John into the car one morning, and he was sick while we were driving back to Allihies, all down the side. Dirty bastard; I was embarrassed. Crows attacked the car. The crows at Allihies were massive and they were pecking the sick off the car. I told John he had better clean it, but that fell on deaf ears. I got nothing. Off we went to Michael Joe's pub again.

We went to the family farm on the second day. Luckily Anthony was there having some dinner. He was off the trawler. We met Ilene, his wife, Mary and John, our cousins. Mary was at a special school in Cork all week because she had Down's Syndrome. She only came home at weekends. John was at school. We chatted with Ilene and Anthony. They said they would come down to the village that night and take us to Castletown for a meal in Murphy's, which they did, and we enjoyed it. They dropped us back at Michael Joe's pub. John got blind drunk, which he did consistently throughout the week. He wasn't sober at all. On the next day, I said to him, 'When are you going to change your clothes?' He and Ryan had the same clothes on as they had arrived in. Tom Cassie said, 'What have you got in the travel bag, John, a bowling ball?'

On day three I went outside after breakfast. I looked up at the windowsill, and I could see four or five empty bottles of Martini. I shouted up at John, 'Get those empty bottles off the windowsill. You're making a right show up of us.' He was lying in bed under the window, and he gave me the V sign. He didn't care; he was in heaven.

Later that day, we decided to go to Castletown to buy plants for the grandparents' grave. These were the grandparents that John lived with when he was over in Ireland, the nearest thing he knew to a mam and dad, who he lived with for five years. The four of us headed for the cemetery, which faced Veronica O'Sullivan's bed and breakfast. Tom said he wouldn't come in, so he waited at the gate. The gates squeaked like something out of a black and white Western. John was steaming drunk and it was only dinner time.

There were no paths in the cemetery; you had to walk carefully around people's graves until you reached the one you wanted. A few years before that, I was in Allihies with cousins from London, Dave and Cathy Hallaran. Before they arrived, we decided to put a headstone on my grandparents' grave. It was left to Harrington who looked after the cemetery to organise it. On our next visit I couldn't find the headstone. I went across with Veronica, who had helped to organise it with Harrington. I asked where the headstone was. She rang Harrington, who came and said, 'Where are you looking?' I showed him. He said, 'Your grandparents are buried over there.' So for all the years we'd been going over and praying, we were at the wrong grave anyway. I apologised.

As we went into the cemetery John was very unsteady. The next thing we knew, he had crashed flat out on Nora Kelly's grave. But as he went down he knocked the arm off the Virgin Mary statue that was on the grave. He lay there with the arm on his lap, with his bottle of Martini. I was fuming. I told him to get up, but he couldn't. Ryan and I had to get him up and steady him. We put the plants on the grave, I said my bits and Ryan said his, and we left John there. God knows what bullshit he was feeding them. I made sure he didn't do any more damage. Tom Cassie was in hysterics. He could hardly stand up, leaning on the squeaky gate. These grandparents were the ones that reared John and he said his own private words to them. But he was more interested in knowing where the next bottle of Martini was coming from.

I'm glad we went. The grave looked well. We headed back into the village to Michael Joe's, but I was still fuming about the damage to the grave. I just prayed that nobody had spotted us there and put the broken arm down to us. We never heard any more about it.

Ryan and John and I had pints of Guinness. I told Michael Joe where we'd been. A guy at the bar said to me, 'Tim Cumba? Is that young John Cumba that the grandparents brought up?' He pointed to John. I said that was him. He said, 'Little John Cumba? The angel?' I thought, *Well, he's not much of an angel.* I didn't tell him he'd just snapped the arm off the Virgin Mary. He said, 'God almighty, he's awful frightening.' John Cumba had certainly left an impression on Allihies! Cumba is the name we have in the village as everyone is called O'Sullivan, so it's a way to distinguish the different families.

At the end of the week, we said our goodbyes and returned to the farm where John spent those few years as a child when Mam couldn't cope. She went back to get him and had to prise him away. The grandparents loved him and wanted John to stay there – they had even promised to leave him the farm in their will.

I said to John, 'Does it bring memories back?'

He said, 'I remember making a snowman here.'

I said, 'If the farm was given to you on a plate again, what would you do?' He made a signal like he was hammering a nail in a wall.

I said, 'What's that?'

He said, 'For sale.'

I said, 'You wouldn't do that. It's our roots.'

But no, that was it. John was never going to go back to his roots.

We dropped the car off. They went up the wall when they saw the state of it. They said, 'We're going to strip this car to clean it, and you're going to be paying. It will come off your credit card.' Kick in the bollocks number one. We got to Cork Airport and I wanted a beautiful Guinness. Tom had found Budweiser because he struggled wicked on Guinness; he had no underpants left, bless him. His stomach wasn't used to it. Michael Joe had got him a case of Budweiser so at least he'd got something to drink. After we dropped the car off John went to the bar. An American film crew started chatting with him but he soon got rid of them with his filthy language. They made out they were getting their plane.

I said, 'It didn't take you long to drive them away.'

He said, 'They've got on the plane.'

I said, 'They fucking ain't, they're round the corner, ordered another round of drinks.'

He was getting louder and louder. I don't know how, but he managed to get hold of my Gold American Express card. I looked up and saw the orders – treble Tia Maria and treble Baileys together in the same glass – and he was putting it on my American Express card. I snatched it back, but he was legless. I said, 'John, get a grip. Quieten down. The noise from you. Everyone is staring at us.' We were going to be boarding soon. In those days, it was a lot laxer, with no seat reservations. You just got on. I said, 'I'm going. They're shouting us now for the plane to Birmingham.' When I got to the check-in, I said, 'Could you call my brother, please, on the tannoy. And my son? They're a bit confused about where they are.' I heard the shout go out. I got on the plane, which then took off. I got up when it was safe and walked around looking for them. I found Tom, who hadn't seen John or Ryan, but then I was told to sit down because of turbulence.

We landed in Birmingham and came through customs. I still didn't see them. Then over the tannoy came, 'Would Tim O'Sullivan go to a courtesy phone.' I picked the phone up.

Pam's voice said, 'You bloody left Ryan in Cork Airport. He couldn't get on the plane. They wouldn't let him and John on.'

As luck would have it, Uncle Anthony and Ilene were at the airport at the same time, going to London, and they slipped Ryan some money. The authorities said, 'You go and sober up, and we will have a look at you, and you can get another flight tonight.' They looked at John and said, 'You, just go.' He asked them to kindly direct him to the bar. They burst out laughing and said, 'You've got no chance.'

So John wandered out and managed to get to Cork City. He was walking down the street, and Mickey Flemming was coming up the other way. He was a Cork City fellow who lived in Leicester. He was pretty well known in Leicester – he played in an Irish band. John said to him, 'Mickey, there is a God.' Mickey Flemming was in some sort of rush, I think. He sort of unloaded John and left him there.

I got home that night and we went to the Addies. The place was packed. All the lads were there, eagerly awaiting to hear about the trip. But I was minus John. I was there with Tom and we had a few drinks and a laugh. It made their night. I said, 'I don't know where John is. I know Ryan is coming back with Uncle Anthony.'

Lord Fife's chauffeur (Lord Fife was chairman of the Co-op) lived in our street. He used to chauffeur me around in his spare time. I got him to pick Ryan up.

Around 12.30 that night, the landline rang. We didn't have mobiles in those days. It was Michael Joe, and he said, 'Jesus Christ, Timmy, you'll never guess who's come through the door – young John.' I was astonished. He had managed to get 150 miles from Cork City, blind drunk. He got the bus from Cork Airport to Bantry and the bus driver was from Allihies and when they got talking he remembered John as a kid. The bus driver ended up giving John a lift back to the village. I asked Michael Joe if he could sort John out. I said I'd make some enquiries to get him back.

I rang him back and said, 'I can get him a flight from Dublin in the morning. But he'll have to get to Dublin,'

Michael Joe said, 'Don't worry, I'll get the lads to drop him off. They go to Dublin on a Wednesday and they'll get him to the airport.' I paid for another flight, and I sent one of my engineers to pick him up. When he came back, he landed in the Addies. The first words out of him were, 'That was expensive, it cost me £600.'

And I said, 'You'd be lucky if you spent £16, you tight bastard.'

The lads asked Tom, 'How was your holiday with the O'Sullivans?'

He said, 'It was the five most horrendous days of my life, but I would never have missed it for the world.' That was our trip and John's homecoming.

Chapter Thirty-Four

He Wasn't Heavy, He Was My Brother

Then at the beginning of 1998, Pam was taking John shopping in Sainsbury's. Suddenly, she heard a crash; John had fallen into a big display of cornflakes. He had virtually passed out, but he wasn't drunk. He had been off the drink for a couple of months. They were very good at Sainsbury's and called an ambulance. Pam went to the hospital with John in the ambulance. She rang me to tell me what was happening; I said I would meet her at the hospital.

After X-rays the doctors said they were not happy. They said they would be keeping him in. I said, 'What do you mean, they're not happy? What is it? He's alright. He's walking. He's talking?' They insisted on keeping him in and doing more tests.' John wasn't bothered. He was off the drink. What started then was three months of tests, tests and more tests. I told the senior doctors that I didn't want any news going to John; I wanted them to tell me first. They would come and inform me. But it was a joke down there. I used to call it the slaughterhouse. I would go down every day, and Lee was on the scene. He was good as gold. He would normally go down after breakfast and spend three hours with John. I would go down after doing my bits with TS and spend a few hours. Then Pam would come in the afternoon. There were no restrictions on visitors. They loved him. He had the place in stitches as usual. We would spend most nights in The Robert Peel, the closest pub to the hospital.

This went on for some time. The nurses said he was better off in the hospital because he got to see the doctors, and once he left, he would just go back into the system. John was getting fed up by now because he had saved a load of dole money that he needed to cash in. But every day was comical. The top doctors would come in during the morning. I would step back, and there would be a group of students. Then one time, one doctor said to another, 'Oh, Simon, I hear your wife got a hole in one on Sunday? Well done to her.'

John said, 'A hole in one? Never mind your wife's fucking hole in one. What about me?' Every day there, he kept that humour going.

There wasn't a day that went by I wouldn't spend an hour or two with John. I would take Mam up two or three times a week when she was up to it. I was waiting for John outside the toilets one morning, and a doctor came up and said, 'Are you John O'Sullivan's next of kin?' I said I was. She introduced herself; I think she was Brazilian. She had a South American accent. She said, 'The tests have come through. Your brother has got emphysema, and it has spread to his brain.' It shocked me. I looked for something to lean on.

The next thing I knew, John had come out of the toilet, doing his trousers up and said, 'So that's it then, the birds nest [rhyming slang for chest] and the napper [brain].' He heard what she said. What a way to find out you were dying. On the toilet. I asked at the desk to see the top man concerning John. They said he would be here that afternoon. I went home and got changed into my suit to meet the top doctor. I had a couple of pints and went back to the hospital.

He was a very nice fella. I said, 'John has been in here for six months on and off, and we've got this.'

He turned and said, 'We had our suspicions in June, Mr O'Sullivan. Would you have liked to know in June that your brother was dying?' I said no. He said, 'Exactly.' I thanked him, and we left it at that.

We were all stunned by John's humour. And he was up. We would go out for a smoke four or five times. He knew a lot of people, coming and going, at the hospital. We just thought he would get mended. But it wasn't to be. They sent him back to the Glenfield. It was like a four-star hotel compared to the Leicester Royal Infirmary, the slaughterhouse. John loved it there. He knew a lot of the nurses from the area. He went back there, and we got on with it.

You couldn't keep his humour down. I'd take Mam up, and he'd say, 'How are you today, Mam?'

She'd say, 'I'm alright, John, the back's playing up.'

And he used to say, 'What age are you now, Mammy?'

She'd say, 'I'm seventy, John.'

He'd say, 'What does it say in the good book? Three score years and ten.'

She'd say, 'Yes, John, that's right.'

He'd say, 'Forty-five, what about me? Why me?'

Mam's mouth would drop open, and she couldn't reply.

Then he'd say, 'I'm going to do you out of that last spot.' Referring to the last space in the cemetery plot.

She looked at me and said, 'Jesus, Timmy, don't let him have the last spot.'

He said, 'No, Mam, I'm going in with Mary, Nora and my dad, and that's that. That's my spot.' John wasn't having any of it. He said, 'That's my spot.'

So John was settled into the Glenfield; it was a different ballgame now. They couldn't give us a time when we could expect it. He was good as gold. We noticed every time we were up there, that a nursing sister named Karen was never far from John. She was there as much as we were. She took a shine to him, which was great. For John to have a sister on the ward who fancied him made his day. It cheered him up. The rest of the nurses knew. They tarted the room up to look like a bedroom on one occasion. John had his own room now. He wasn't on a ward. God knows what went on, but things weren't looking good. This went on for about a month. John had nightmares and fits started to kick in. He was on morphine. Karen took full control, which took a lot of the pressure off us. We didn't know what was going on in the hospital, but she knew all the ins and outs. I remember she rang to say he was having terrible fits. We went down there. They had filled him full of morphine.

The rest of the family arrived. Young John arrived. I had Mam there, Pam, Ryan, and Kelly. Paddy arrived. Young Johnny's mother was there, in the room. The breathing got terrible. I thought, *This is it.* I said to the nurse, 'Can we have a priest?' They said they would organise it. To me, that was it. The priest arrived. The breathing didn't get any better, and he gave John the Last Rites.

John came round and opened his eyes. The priest was giving him a blessing, and he pushed the priest's face out of the way. It horrified him. He thought he had died and was in the wrong place. He was expecting hell and he'd landed in heaven. And then he came around a bit and started talking. He said to Ann, 'You're still the best looking girl in Leicester,' which we thought was nice.

As the day went on and the afternoon dragged, it was very hot in that room. There were seventeen people in the room. Ryan turned up. He had come back from Holland, where he was studying for his degree. He was at university now. You wouldn't get away with that today. The breathing got better and better. I said to the family, 'He's going nowhere.' So off to the pub we headed, me, Ryan, Lee and young John. We left the girls there to look after things.

When we went in the next day, I didn't know what we would find, but there he was, sitting up in bed. He'd just finished a big breakfast, happy as Larry. He told me he was getting engaged to Karen, which we were all happy for. We decided to go out. Because there was nothing they could do for John now. He was able. He could walk as long as he got the morphine for the pain. Pam organised a new set of clothes. Ryan gave him a pair of Timberland boots. I said to John, 'I haven't seen you look this smart in years.'

John said, 'I want burying in these clothes.' At the same time, 'He ain't heavy, he's my brother' by the Hollies was playing on the radio in his room. He said he wanted that song played at his funeral. We arranged for a meal at the Cedars in Evington, an engagement party. Pam's sisters were there and her nieces. We all ended up there, and at the end, I got John and myself a pint of Guinness. I sat next to him. He couldn't finish his drink. He knew then he'd started to look bad. It was kicking in quickly. Rather than being a celebration, it turned into a mini wake, like we'd half buried him.

We all knew it was just a matter of time. The next thing was to get John into the hospice Loros. We had a couple of neighbours from our street that had been in there for months and were still hanging on. The next week flew by. We were still going up to the hospital. One morning I'd got up there early at eight thirty. John was asleep. I knelt beside the bed and started praying to God to help him. I was crying and his hand came down on top of my head, and he said, 'Don't worry, Tadhgeen, I'll be alright.' And then he dropped back to sleep.

Lee turned up, and we spent a couple of hours. Some days he was good. They had to fit a bottle to him, with a tube attached to his lung. It drained all the fluids and the shit off his lung. I took John out to the restaurant. He put the bottle on the table and I was expected to eat my meal, staring at this bottle of fluid. Everyone else there was as well. It was one of those restaurants where everyone ate together, the surgeons, doctors, porters. I say to him, 'John, will you put that on the floor out of the way. It's fucking disgusting.'

He said, 'Fuck them. I want them to see what agony I'm going through.' You could see people looking over, shaking their heads and pushing their dinners away. He wasn't bothered. The call came to get John into Loros on Friday morning. I was tied up with TS Refrigeration, so Lee said he would sort it.

Lee went down to the hospital. He was going to give him a lift to the hospice. Lee rang me from Loros. John was outside; he wasn't having it. He knew that when he went through the door, he was finished. We didn't know much about Loros. It was new to us – it was a place for people to go towards the end of their lives. Eventually, he got him in. The people there were just five star.

When I arrived, he was out cold, unconscious. Pam went up the wall and asked why he was out cold. They said, 'We always ask if they are in pain, and do they want us to give them something for it.'

I said, 'Who gives the OK to give him something?' Morphine, it would be. I said, 'I'm his next of kin.' They pointed over to Karen.

Pam and I were furious. We calmed down eventually and I got somebody to pick Mam up. That was Friday night. The next day, Saturday, I visited. I knew then with the breathing, the rattle. Every minute it was a waiting game. The word went out, and I let everyone know that if they wanted to say their farewells to John, to come and say them today because he wouldn't last much longer. The lads, fair play. Ann turned up. We were all in and out. They had a smoking room in Loros. I remember going into it. There was a woman who was a patient there. She wasn't well, but she was a chain smoker, so they had moved her bed into the smoking room. And that's all she did, read and smoke. It was great. Anything you wanted, you could get there. Even a drink. But John was way past that.

I went home and had something to eat. I tried to sleep. That night we got a phone call saying his breathing was getting worse. I rang Mam. Mam was up there in the daytime with me. We were in the room. He went about an hour after. A quarter to ten on Saturday night, it was 14 November 1998. I remember it well. Pam was there. I was there, Kelly; Johnny was there. There was a good crowd. I said my prayers and kissed him. I went outside for a smoke. I was leaning on a fence, and I saw a star shoot across the sky. Heading westward, towards Ireland. I convinced myself that it was John. I went back in. They were all still there, quiet, crying. I said, 'Come on, he's gone. He's gone. The spirit has gone. It's only the body left.'

I left and went down to the Addies, where we had a good drink. The next day we had to try to organise the funeral. We had Father Lynch at St Pat's at the time. He liked a drink, did Father Lynch. No offence, fair play to him. But I could not track him down on the Monday. A good family friend, Mick Byrnes popped up. He said he would track him down. So we managed to get Father Lynch. I went to see him. I was with him for around half an hour. My phone rang. I excused myself and answered it. It was the *Leicester Mercury*. They said, 'Hello, are you, Tim O'Sullivan?'

I said, 'Yes.'

They said, 'Was it your brother John O'Sullivan who died recently?'

I said, 'Yes, it was.'

They said, 'We've had hundreds of people sending in their condolences. We've never seen anything like it. Was he famous?'
I said, 'Well, yes.'
They said, 'What for? Was he a sportsman or an entertainer?'
I said, 'No. No, he was just my brother.'
The next night and the following nights, there were record numbers of notices in the *Leicester Mercury*, considering to put a minimum one-liner in would cost £20 in those days. To put a little four-liner in would cost £40. Fair play to them.

Anyway, we got the funeral arranged for Friday. It was busy seeing people arranging it. I got the same undertakers who did for my dad. It was set for Friday at St Pat's church. We already had the plot; I'd bought a fresh plot – a three berth. For me, John, and Pam. That resolved the arguments over the last spot in the family plot.

On the day of the funeral, Dave and Cathy Halloran came up from London. People came over from Ireland. Then ten o'clock at St Pat's. I would give John a president's funeral. It wasn't going to be a pauper's funeral like my sister Mary's. We had five cars for all the family. The convoy headed for St Pat's. As we pulled into Beaumont Leys Lane, there were hundreds, absolutely hundreds of people queued up outside St Pat's. It took my breath away to see them. We pulled up outside the church.

I'd organised the bagpiper, Andy Maccie, whose family were from Donegal. When everyone was in the church it was rammed. People were standing. I knew St Pat's held one thousand people. There were people standing in the aisles, and people still outside. We couldn't get them in. The priest was gobsmacked. He had never seen that many people in the church. Six of us carried John in, me, his son Jonny, Lee, Ryan, my nephew Paddy and my niece's partner Adrian. The coffin weighed a ton; John was a huge man anyway, but people who had visited him to say their farewells had put cans of Guinness in, so all that extra weight and the rattling of the tins made it even harder.

I got up and gave a eulogy, which people liked. After the Mass, we went up to the cemetery and buried him. We had the wake at the Irish Centre on Gipsy Lane.

It would have been an expensive day for the lads, getting to St Pat's, up to the cemetery, and the Irish Centre. So I put two double-decker buses on. I'd started drinking at half seven that morning – cans of Guinness. By the time I walked home at midnight from the Addies Bar with Pam, stone-cold sober, I had drunk a good thirty pints. But I knew about the thirty pints the next day when Bogside and I went up to tidy up the grave.

After John's funeral, everything went quiet. Except for drink. That's what I did. I'd get up, have my Weetabix, go down the Standard, drink until two-ish. Go home, go to bed, get up, pick at my dinner, and go down the Addies. Come home, go to bed, and listen to records. And that went on. Christmas came and went. The New Year didn't mean anything. Pam tried to do her best. Fair play to Kevin. He kept everything going at TS.

January came and went. February came and went. It was the same pattern. Going for drinks, morning and night. I would see Mam twice a week through all of this. She didn't have the same old fire. She found it hard. She'd buried two kids. But we tried to bond. We managed.

I got a phone call. It was Mother's Day, 14 March 1999 on the Sunday. I planned to see Mam at Mass. But I got a phone call at seven in the morning from Social Services. We had a panic phone for Mam in her house. They rang me and said, 'Can you go to your mother's house? There's an ambulance on the way.' They were very rude and matter of fact.

I got Pam, and we drove up there. When we arrived, there was a PC in the house and a police car outside. He said, 'Come in, Tim, sit down.'

I said, 'She's gone?'

He said, 'Yes, she has.'

I went up, and she was lying in bed, peaceful as anything. She'd gone in the night. It was exactly four months to the day since John had died. I kissed her. She was coldish. I came down and Pam made a cup of tea for us and the policeman. We had to wait for the doctor. I was chatting with the young copper, McLaughlan. His parents were Irish. I was telling him bits of my story and Mam's life. The doctor came. Pam had rung Bonnie, Johnny and all of them. Bonnie turned up, from Ashby, bless her. And Paddy. That was Sunday dinner. There was only one place for me, and that was the pub.

We buried Mam at St Pat's. We had a quiet do. The funeral was paid for with Mam's insurance. That was what she wanted, and she said whatever was left to drink it. Well, low and behold, we did. The tab was over £400. And there was £300 left after the funeral. Mam's friends, the old Irish biddies from church, were there, and a good few of my friends. So, we put Mam to bed. And it was back to the pub, and the drinking, for me. We went out for St Pat's Day three days later.

So it was back to the drink and the routine. Breakfast. Walk into town. The Standard, half-ten. Half-two, home. I wasn't the best. The Guinness was getting the best of me.

Chris Griffin, my old schoolmate from St Pat's and English Martyrs, rang me from Australia when he found out about Mam. He said, 'Right, Tim, I want you in my back garden for the millennium. The world is getting ready for this big massive party for the new century.' So I started to plan. Chris was in Perth, Australia. And

I thought, that's it, I've got to snap out of this. I slowly got back into the grind at TS and went back into everything. I booked the flights to see Chris in Perth. We decided we would have five days in Singapore on the way out, then three weeks in Perth, and five days in Hong Kong on the return journey. We went, and Chris was sound. It was great. We saw the New Year in and saw the new century in. It was a bit of a flop, but that's how it was worldwide. I came back, and I thought, a new century, let's bash on. Move on. And that was that.

Tim's last drink with his brother John before he died

A triute to John to mark the 20th anniversary of his death

Chapter Thirty-Five

Fresh Beginnings

In 2016 I noticed that I was going to the toilet a lot at night. I went to the doctor to get a check up. An appointment was made at Leicester General. When we got there, the nursing staff were fuming apparently a new Doctor turned up on his first day three hours late. So my 2 pm appointment was pushed back till 5 pm. When I went in, I was a bag of nerves, there was an African so-called doctor and a pretty Muslim nurse. The doctor he said to me "come in", he checked his notes and without even looking up he said "you've got prostate cancer". And in the next breath he said "the worst things for it are smoking, caffeine and drinking alcohol". Well, my world froze. To be told you've got cancer, and then that you can't drink or smoke. Then the next thing, he told me to bend over a couch and he rammed his nine-inch finger up my bottom and then sent me on my way. I later found out that he was a fraud and that the hospital had sacked him. Finding that out, I would have liked to have been the doctor and rammed a stick of rock up his arse and told him that he had prostate cancer. From there I went through my private healthcare. I met a brilliant fella. Professor Khan. He did a test on me. He told me I was count 6.5.

He said he doesn't worry until it gets into the teens. He said just get on with your life and I will see you in six months. He didn't mention drinking or smoking. Eventually, with the radiology, my count now is 0.4, which is nothing. And it has been like that since.

After thirty-five years at TS Refrigeration, I had built one of the top commercial refrigeration businesses in Leicester. Over the years I had given my faithful engineer Kevin Hallam forty-nine per cent of the business at no charge. When it came time for me to step away, my accountant valued the business at £345,000, and I sold the remainder to Kevin at a reduced cost to acknowledge his loyalty and commitment to me and the business for more than thirty years. Being semi-retired, I decided to buy the Adventures and am still the owner. This turned out to be a great investment and I added to that by buying more commercial and residential properties around the local area.

But I did decide to sell my Mam's house. I wasn't interested in profiting out of it. When I sold it, I took what I had paid for it and some more for what I spent doing it up, and I shared the rest with the grandchildren. Jonny was looking at buying the council house he was in, so I handed him a chunk towards that. Paddy had just got his garden sorted out, so I gave him some towards that. Bonnie and Adrian, they were desperate to get her own home, so I said I would help her with the deposit. She ended up buying a beautiful house from the estate in Ashby. Not long after that, Bonnie gave birth to a little girl called Keely. We all jumped in the Merc and went off to Ashby to see her. Later they had a son called Jordan. Bonnie ended up being a teaching assistant. She might have been old before her time having brought Paddy up. But Bonnie was an angel. Mary would have been so proud of her.

Paddy never went back to the glue but he'd have the odd smoke of the gear here and there. But he did get a taste for the beer. The drinking got worse over time. But he snapped out of it some time in 2008 and he's never touched a drop of drink since. That was a turning point for him. He's got a son, Malachy, who we watched grow up. It seemed Malachy would be the only one from all the family that would carry on the O'Sullivan name. The relationship with Malachy's mother didn't work out, but he is doing very well now. He talks his head off, he never stops, but I am proud of him.

Our kids both turned out well too. Ryan soon figured out that he'd rather use his brain than his muscles, that's how he was. He left school and went to university. He finished his degree in Holland, in Arnhem; he was the first O'Sullivan to get a university degree. He then did his Masters in Toronto and we went to see him over there and had a great time, and we also took Pam's niece, Donna. Ryan went on to complete his Doctorate, so he's Dr O'Sullivan now. He is married to a lovely French lady called Elisabeth and they have a daughter, Charlotte; they live in the South of France.

Kelly turned into a beautiful young lady. She actually won the 'Rose of Tralee' when it came to Leicester. She didn't have a boyfriend at the time so I got to have the dance with her at the end. That was a very proud moment for me. I ended up falling out with the organisers because in the end I felt it became too elitist with expensive tickets and guests needing tuxedos and ballgowns; there were too many barriers for working-class people to enter.

Kelly stayed with the animals. She started as a veterinary nurse in a surgery in Leicester, then she moved down to London where she's the manager of a veterinary surgery and has been working there for a good few years. She has made her life in London; she got married to an Essex guy called Matt. The wedding was at St Patrick's Church in Leicester, and walking her down the aisle was one of my proudest moments. It made a change from carrying family coffins down the aisle. It was a big wedding with all the family together. She has two children, Avalon and Cillian.

Chapter Thirty-Six

Our History, Our Inheritance

It took decades to step back and get a sense of perspective on my past. I have come a long way from the taunted lad in hand-me-down clothes raised by a lone parent who struggled to make ends meet. Mam worked at poorly paid menial jobs to support her three children. She longed for us to respect our Irish heritage and keep the faith.

My memories are vivid of those early years, but narrowed by a child's-eye view. Only when I began to raise my own children did I get an inkling of what she must have gone through. I had Pam, a fantastic supportive wife and mother, to share my life with. Mam had been given over to the nuns in an orphanage so young. She had no memory of her own mother, no role model to follow, no idea how to run a home. No training to earn a decent wage.

Rescued by Norah from the orphanage, Mam thought she'd found her hero in my dad. He was no John Wayne, just a big Irishman terrified of marriage with no idea how to raise a family. Not a bad man, not exactly reliable, but a bit broken by life too.

Yes, we three children were cold, often hungry, and left on our own when Mam went out to work. But we always knew we were fiercely loved, never abandoned. My toughest memories replay with regret, for broken lives I couldn't mend.

Why did I make it through when my siblings didn't? Hell, I'm no angel. I've made big mistakes, spent time inside, shamed Mam. At first I had to eke out a way to survive – shoplifting apples to stave off hunger, standing up to bullies, later joining their gang for security. Not a good move, but a very necessary one.

I found out the system isn't all bad. I chose to wear the glasses I obviously needed. I stuck with school. My brother refused, choosing to be a great entertainer, but illiterate. My sister loathed the system, opting out, feeling the world owed her a much better deal. I thrived thanks to free school meals and free school uniforms. I found various jobs before I left school, figured out the fiddles, and pretty soon knew I was damn good at managing systems and rotas. A new headmaster at school sensed I had potential.

By eighteen, I was already a dad, had been dumped, and had a criminal record. It wasn't looking good. I was moving with a rough crowd of hooligans. John and Mary were already into drink and drugs, usually refusing help. A wise social worker kept me level-headed. A priest kept us from being evicted. Unlike my siblings, I kept on learning, kept on at work.

I became trusted, reliable, an earner, helping to ease Mam's burden. Then I met Pam. She was too good to lose; she deserved proper courting. Mam loved her. She was hard-working, clever, and gorgeous. She believed in me, and life has never been the same since. She juggled three jobs when I decided to go independent and start my own business. As my siblings spiralled into alcoholism and addiction, she kept our family steady, and supported Mam throughout. Pam understood my need to bring Lee into our family, to help him know his real father.

The church has stood by us in our tragedies, and buried Mary and Nora when they were penniless, given them an honourable send-off. Eventually, Nora, Mary, Dad and Mam were buried in the plot I later purchased from St Patrick's. Yes, I was a mess after I lost them all, awash in the Guinness for months. Out of it.

But I managed to pull myself back from the brink. It wasn't easy. We are all fragile, easily broken. The grandkids need to know the facts and face the brutal unvarnished truth. This too is your heritage.

Yes, Mam would be proud that I have made something of my life, that we have a very decent standard of living and money in the bank. That is well and good, but what Mam would really feel proud about is that I have provided steadfast support and care for our wider family network, giving them a name, an identity they can hold with pride in spite of the tragedies.

Mam, your fierce love lives on in us.

Tim, and John's son Johnny holding a cheque showing money raised for LOROS, where John died

22

ADVERTISING FEATURE

TOASTING THEIR SUCCESS: (l-r) Darren Horner, Tim Smith, Amy Calver, Danny Herbert, manager Kevin Hallam, Pamela O'Sullivan and managing director Tim O'Sullivan

IN IT TOGETHER: Tim and Kevin (right of picture) encourage team work and a friendly approach

AT YOUR SERVICE: TS Refrigeration has a fleet of four vans

Silver jubilee for TS Refrigeration

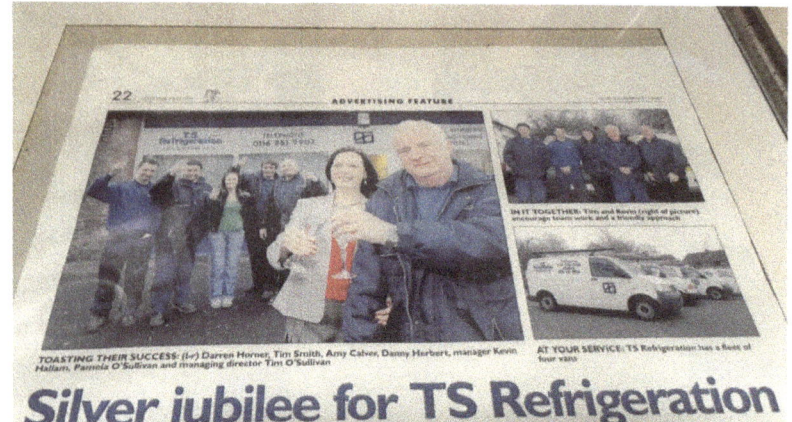

Celebrations for 25 years of TS Refrigeration

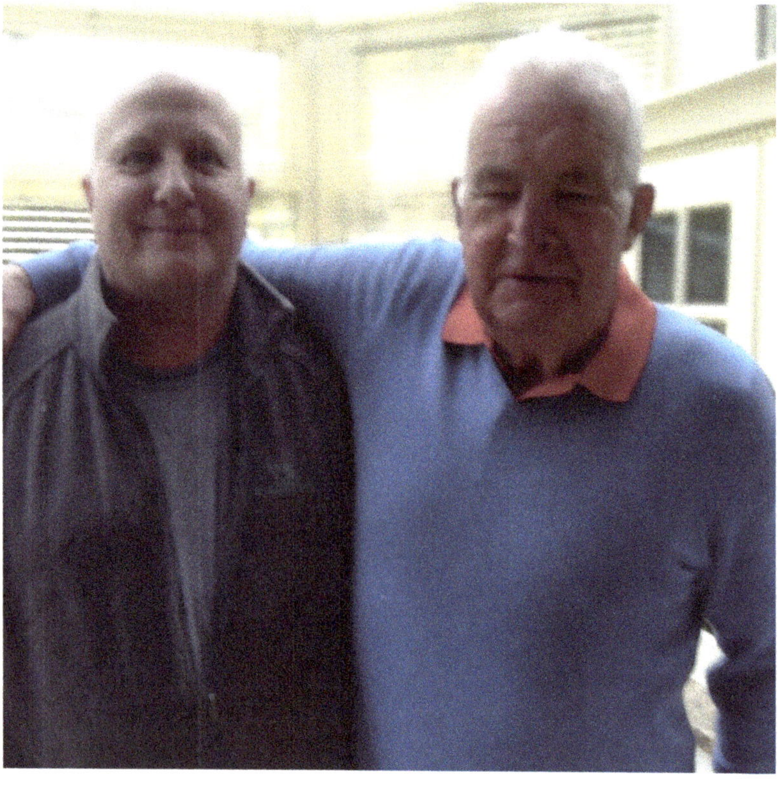

Tim and Kevin Hallam who now owns TS Refrigeration

TIM'S FAMILY ALBUM

Lee, Johnny, Ryan, Paddy, Bonnie, Nanna and Kelly on a family night out

Tim and Pam's son, Ryan, wife Elisabeth and daughter Charlotte

Tim's nephew Paddy, with his son Malachy

Tim's niece Bonnie with Adrian, Keeley and Jordan

Tim's Auntie Bridget

John's son Johnny with partner Michelle, and their daughters Maihiri, Macey and Farrah

*Pam and Tim's daughter Kelly, husband Matt,
and their children Avalon and Cillian*

Pam's sister Chriss and Denise

Kelly, Lee and Ryan

Tim with his son Lee

Mary, Mam and Bonnie

www.ingramcontent.com/pod-product-compliance
Lightning Source LLC
Chambersburg PA
CBHW061146170426
43209CB00011B/1571